The Lesser Key of Solomon
—or—
Goetia
—The Book of Evil Spirits—

A MODERN RENDERING OF
THE 17TH CENTURY GRIMOIRE
With an Introduction, Commentary & Appendix By
DENNIS LOGAN

Aleister Crowley
S.L. MacGregor Mathers
L.W. DeLaurence

Copyright, 2025

By

Penemue Media LLC

All Rights Reserved

ISBN: 978-1-964297-04-0

SPECIAL NOTICE

This edition of The Lesser Key of Solomon is a restored and enhanced facsimile of a public domain text, with original commentary, essays, and design elements added by the publisher. While the core text remains in the public domain, this edition—including all formatting, annotations, and supplemental content—is copyright © 2025 Penemue Media LLC. No part of this edition may be reproduced or distributed without written permission, except for brief excerpts under fair use.

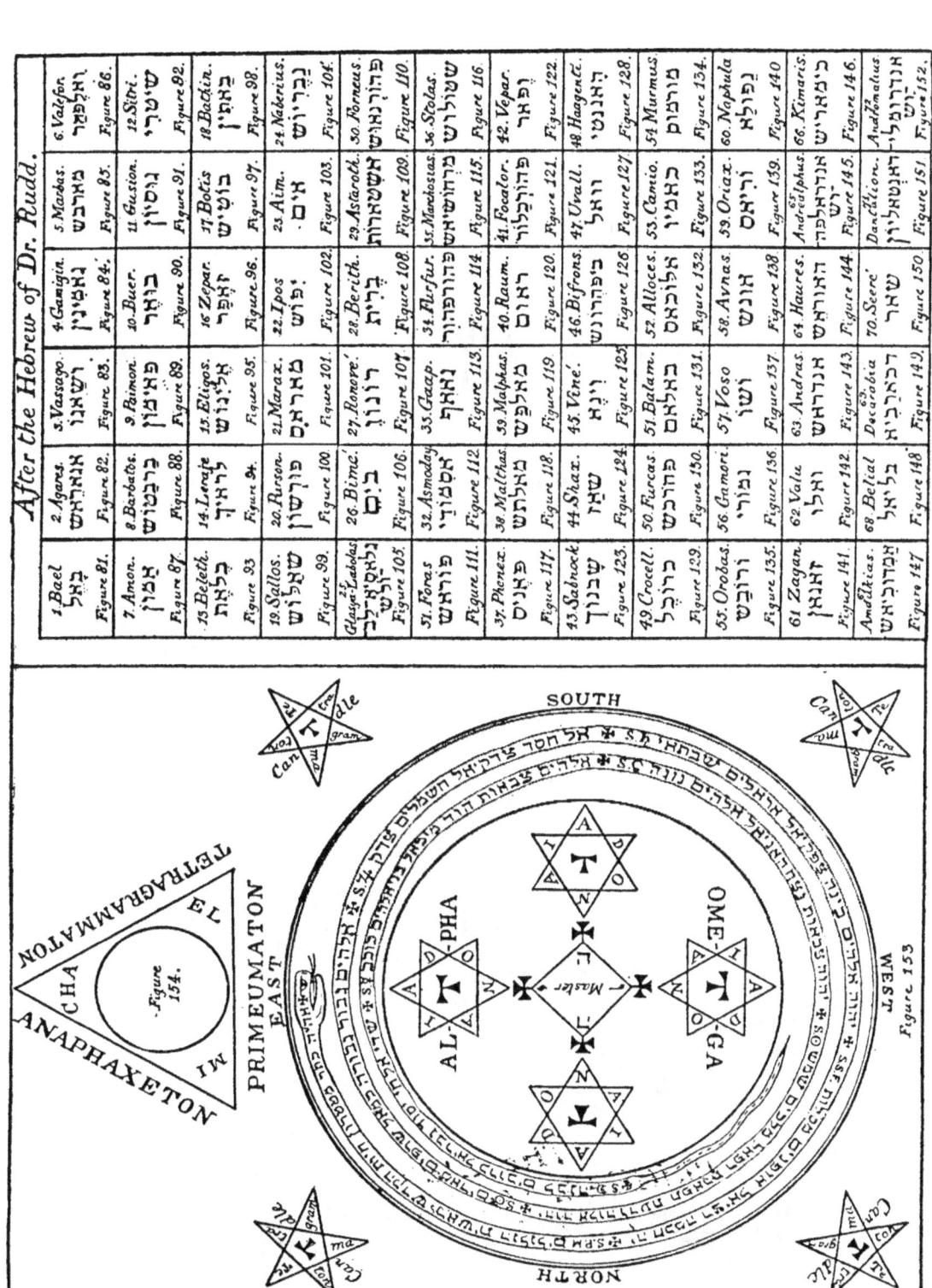

Figure 153.

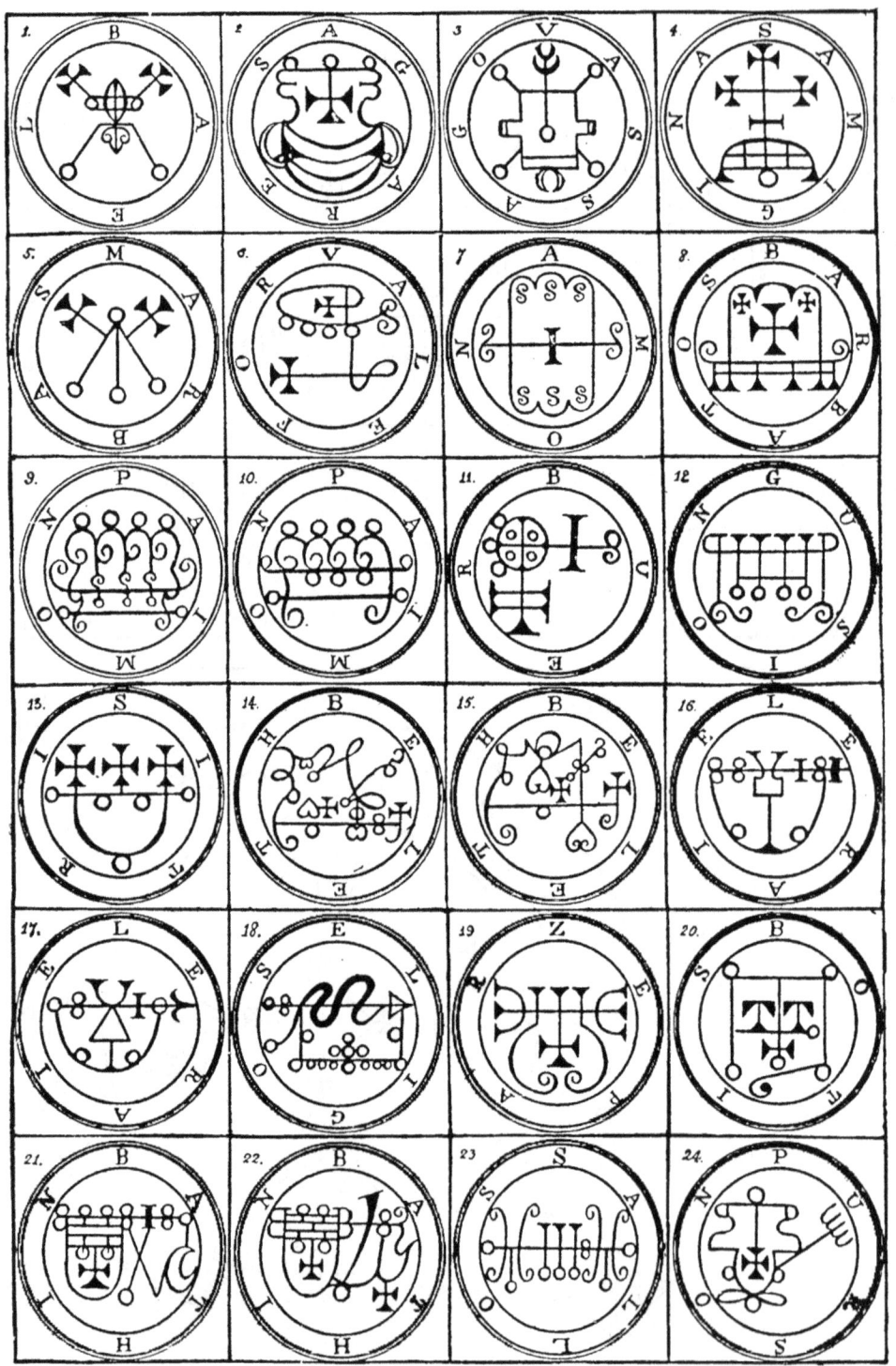

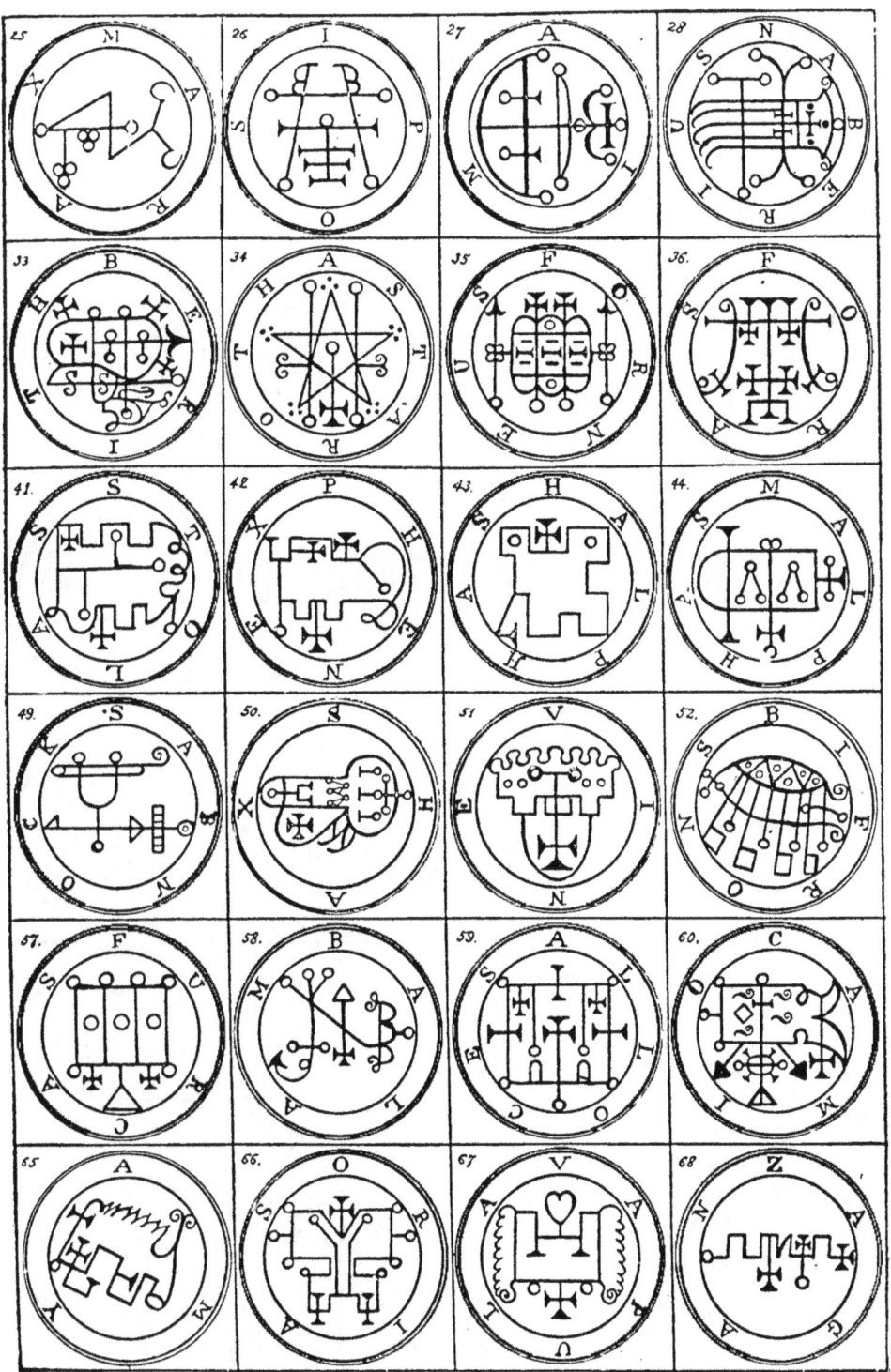

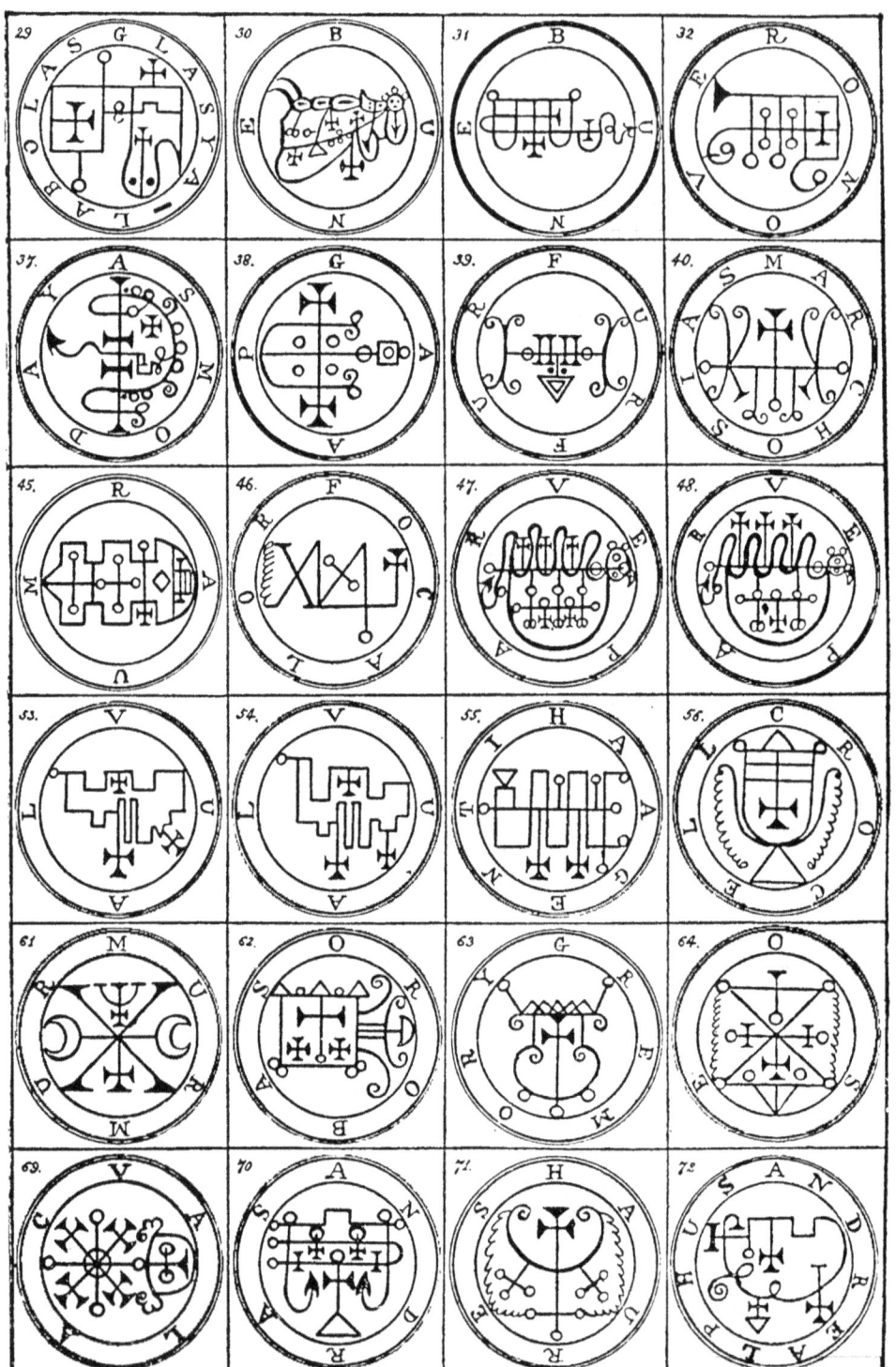

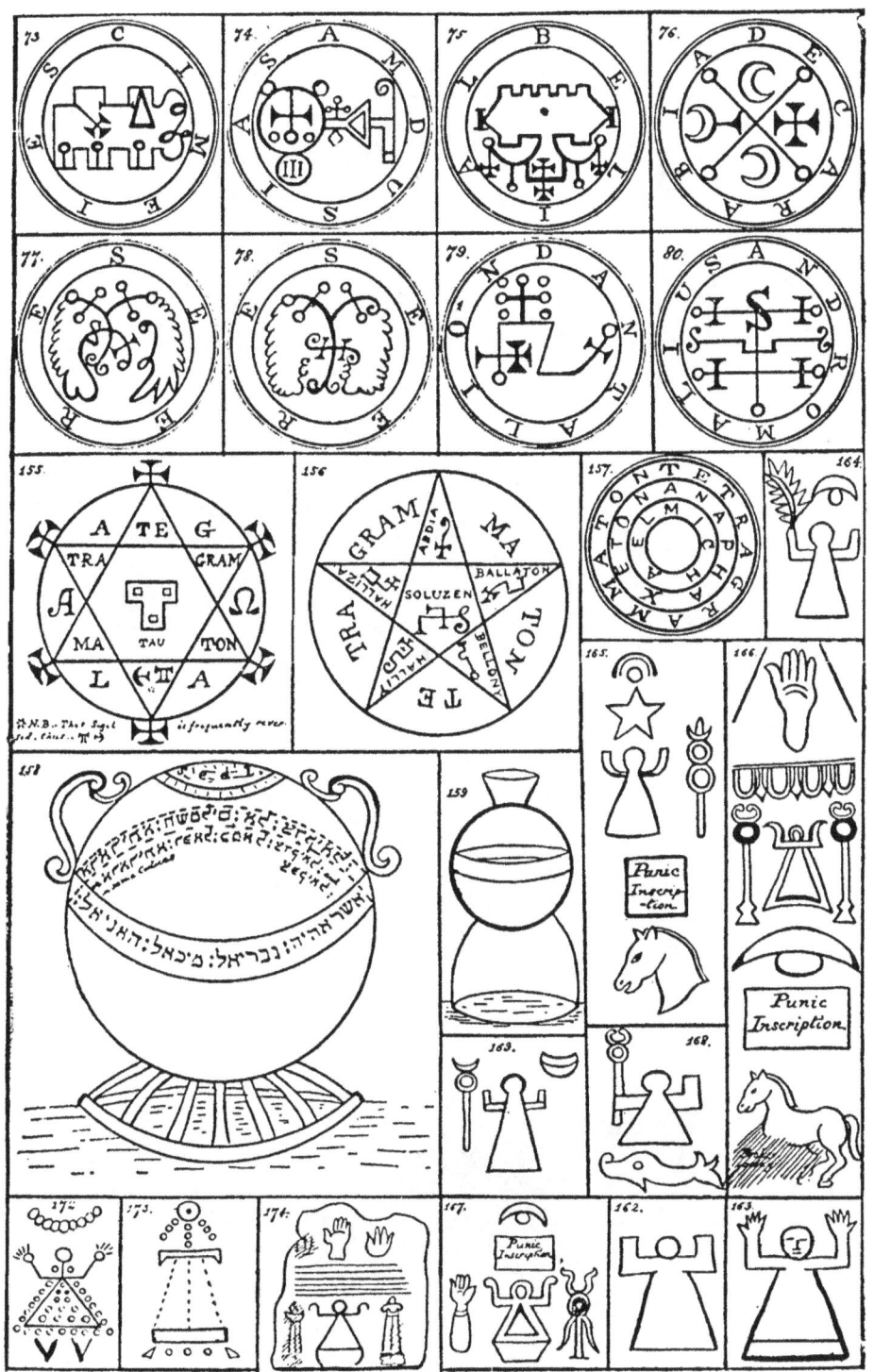

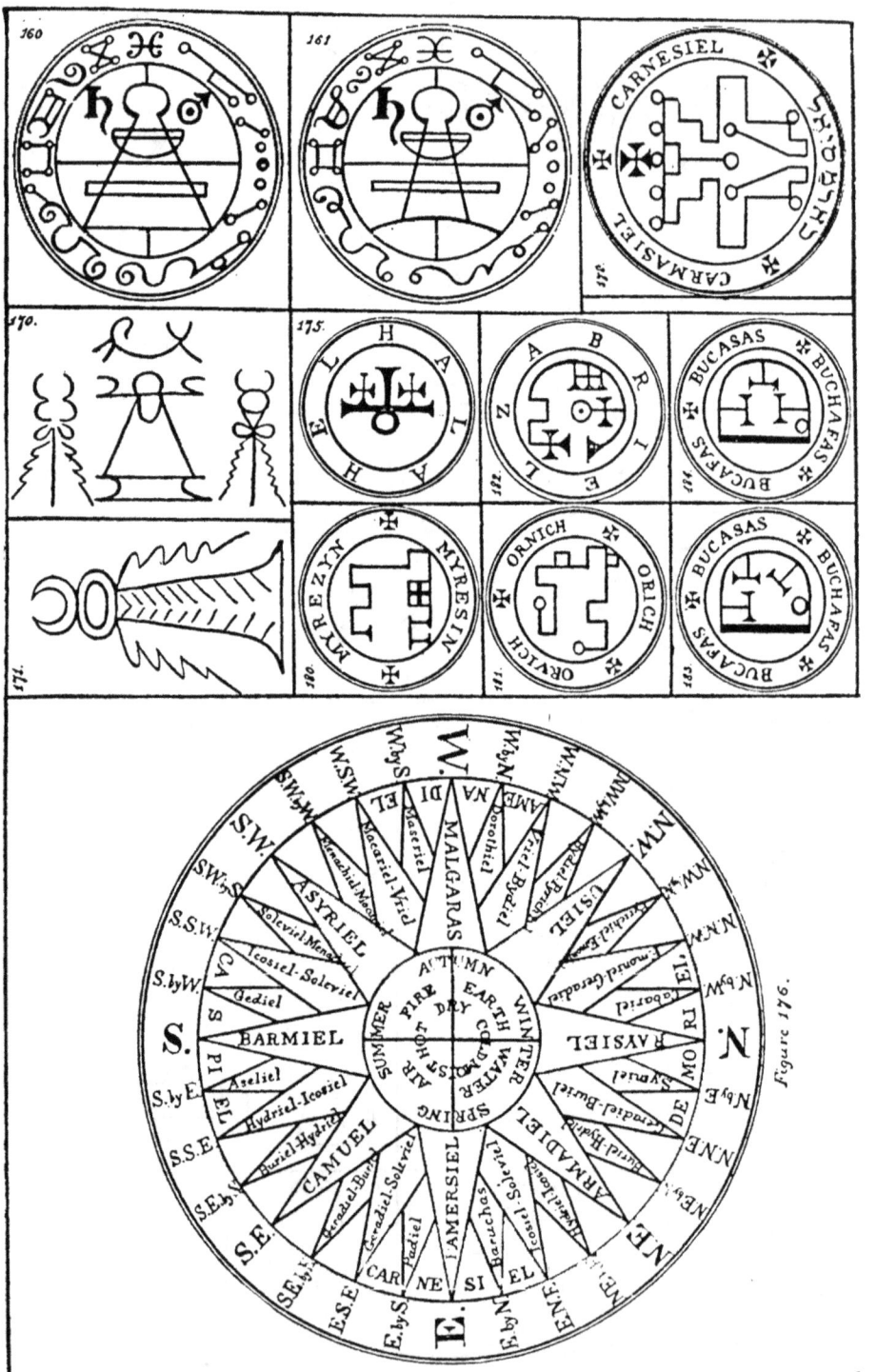

Figure 146.

Goetia
The Lesser Key Of
King Solomon

Introduction to The Lesser Key of Solomon

The Lesser Key of Solomon, or *Lemegeton Clavicula Salomonis*, is a composite grimoire that occupies a central position in the literature of ceremonial magic. Compiled in the seventeenth century from earlier sources, the text is divided into five books: *Goetia, Theurgia-Goetia, Ars Paulina, Ars Almadel,* and *Ars Notoria.* The version here presented is a facsimile of the English translation attributed to S.L. MacGregor Mathers and Aleister Crowley, and later pirated through the commercial editions of L.W. de Laurence in the early twentieth century.

This edition has been cleaned of advertising and self-promotional material from *De Laurence, Scott and Co.*, a firm whose name has become synonymous with exploitative occult publishing. There is no association between that firm and the present publisher. All editorial decisions made here aim to retain the scholarly and magical value of the text while clarifying its cultural and historical context for contemporary readers.

The Lesser Key in Relation to the Greater Key

For the neophyte, it is essential to understand the distinction between *The Lesser Key of Solomon* and its companion text, *The Greater Key of Solomon*. The *Greater Key* is a ritual manual of high magic, focused on consecration, planetary alignment, and the invocation of angelic powers in harmony with divine will. Its tone is devotional and aspirational.

The Lesser Key, by contrast, is operative and immediate. The *Goetia*, the first and most famous section, offers descriptions and sigils of 72 spirits said to have been bound by King Solomon. These spirits—often infernal, rebellious, or ambivalent—are conjured not through worship, but command. The magician, acting with authority derived from divine names and ritual preparation, seeks to compel cooperation through forceful invocation.

To the adept, the distinction is one of intent and metaphysics: the *Greater Key* seeks ascent toward divine communion; the *Lesser* manages engagement with intermediary—and often morally ambiguous—entities. One elevates; the other negotiates.

On Pseudepigrapha and Attribution

Like its companion volume, the *Lesser Key* is a pseudepigraphon—a work falsely attributed to a biblical figure, in this case Solomon, to lend it spiritual weight. Its real origins lie in the Renaissance grimoires of Christian and Jewish magicians, heavily influenced by earlier Arabic texts on spirit hierarchies and planetary forces. While framed as an ancient manual, it is in fact a syncretic artifact—part folklore, part mysticism, part theological speculation.

Understanding this provenance is vital. These books were never canonical scripture, nor were they revealed truths from a singular origin. Rather, they are the residue of centuries of magical experimentation, layered with theological disguise.

Mental Health and the Risks of Delusion

Modern practitioners must approach this material with clear boundaries between inner experience and external reality. As early as the sixteenth century, physician Johan Weyer warned that those believed to be possessed were often suffering from untreated mental illness. In our time, this insight is not only relevant—it is essential. Psychiatry has since evolved far more rigorous diagnostic tools, and what was once called demonic may now fall under categories such as schizophrenia, bipolar disorder, or dissociative identity disorder.

Aleister Crowley himself stated that the 72 spirits of the *Goetia* correspond to different regions or tendencies of the human mind. To work with them is to invoke latent aspects of one's own psyche—often dark, fractured, and unintegrated. When improperly handled, this process may trigger spiritual psychosis, egotism, narcissistic dissociation, sociopathic tendencies, manic ideation, lethargy, or deep melancholy. It is not uncommon for those immersed in such workings to develop delusions of grandeur or persecution, mistaking psychological disintegration for magical attainment.

This risk is compounded by external scrutiny. Practicing these rites publicly or speaking too openly about them can lead to social alienation, involuntary psychiatric intervention, and legal ramifications. Once someone has been institutionalized or branded mentally ill, that label becomes exceedingly difficult to remove—

regardless of circumstance. Discretion, therefore, is not merely a magical virtue but a social necessity.

Owen Davies, in his seminal *Grimoires: A History of Magic Books*, notes that in early twentieth-century Jamaica, over 80% of individuals admitted to psychiatric institutions for schizophrenia or bipolar disorder were found to possess copies of de Laurence's books when their homes were searched. While causality cannot be assumed, the correlation is worth deep reflection: the seductive promises of power, when combined with psychological vulnerability and spiritual confusion, can lead to tragic outcomes.

Those who undertake this work must do so with restraint, silence, and a firm anchor in reality. Inner exploration must be balanced by outer functionality, or the consequences may outweigh the insights.

On the Marketplace of Magic

As with all ceremonial traditions, there exists a thriving market for magical paraphernalia. Every tool described in this book—from brass vessels to parchment pentacles, from lion-skin belts to incense of astrological timing—can be purchased, often at inflated cost and questionable authenticity. The magician must ask: are these tools truly necessary, or are they commodified proxies for inner discipline?

In this regard, Anton LaVey's insight is relevant: "You can cast a spell and hope it works, or punch someone in the face and get immediate gratification." While not advocating violence, the principle holds—magic must never be a substitute for direct action or personal agency. The rituals of the *Lemegeton* were once performed in solitude by scholars and mystics; today, they are often ritualized by consumers seeking power. Do not mistake performance for transformation.

A Warning Regarding Public Use of Sigils and Seals

A serious admonition must be given: the sigils and seals contained within the *Lesser Key* are not ornaments, nor are they meant to be displayed in public or commercialized settings. Their use is intended to be secret, personal, and ritualistically guarded. To emblazon them on clothing, websites, or business logos is to profane their symbolic structure and misunderstand their function.

Wearing or displaying these sigils carelessly may attract attention, but not the kind the magician seeks. If you encounter these symbols in popular culture, social media, or commercial spaces, take it not as an invitation to dig deeper—but as a sign to walk away. It often reveals more about the ignorance or instability of the wearer than any arcane power they claim to wield.

On Cultic Appropriation and De Laurence's Legacy

Texts such as this have long been exploited by self-styled gurus, cult leaders, and opportunists. The history of L.W. de Laurence illustrates this risk. While he played a role in preserving and spreading magical texts, he also blurred the line between publication and manipulation. De Laurence was repeatedly accused of fraud, copyright theft, and spiritual exploitation—especially among colonial subjects in India and the Caribbean, where his works were marketed as instant pathways to wealth, success, or domination.

Be wary of anyone treating this text as infallible doctrine. It is a symbolic manual, not a belief system. The moment it is framed as exclusive gnosis requiring allegiance or financial contribution, you are no longer in the domain of magic—you are in the domain of cult.

On This Edition

To enhance clarity and accessibility, this edition includes every biblical reference cited in the *Lemegeton*, reproduced in full in the appendix. This eliminates the need to consult external volumes and grounds the text more firmly within its Judeo-Christian narrative structure.

May this work serve not as a delusion or dogma, but as a structured mirror for those with the strength to face themselves—and the wisdom to walk away when the mirror darkens.

-Dennis Logan

Richmond, VA USA

7/14/2025

Goetia
The Lesser Key Of King Solomon

ΕΠΙΚΑΛΟΥΜΑΙ ΣΕ ΤΟΝ ΕΝ ΤΩ ΚΕΝΕΩ ΠΝΕΥΜΑΤΙ, ΔΕΙΝΟΝ, ΑΟΡΑΤΟΝ, ΠΑΝΟΤΡΑΤΟΡΑ, ΘΕΟΝ ΘΕΩΝ, ΦΘΕΡΟΠΟΙΟΝ, ΚΑΙ ΕΠΗΜΟΠΟΙΝ, Ο ΜΙΣΩΝ ΟΙΚΙΑΝ ΕΥΣΤΑΘΟΥΣΑΝ, ΩΣ ΕΞΕΒΡΑΣΘΗΣ ΕΚ ΤΗΣ ΑΙΓΥΠΤΙΟΥ ΚΑΙ ΕΞΩ ΧΩΡΑΣ.

ΕΠΟΝΟΜΑΣΘΗΣ Ο ΠΑΝΤΑ ΠΗΣΣΩΝ ΚΑΙ ΜΗ ΝΙΚΩΜΕΝΟΣ.

ΕΠΙΚΑΛΟΥΜΑΙ ΣΕ ΤΥΦΩΝ ΣΗΘ ΤΑΣ ΣΑΣ ΜΑΤΡΕΙΑΣ ΕΠΙΤΕΛΩ, ΟΤΙ ΕΠΙΚΑΛΟΥΜΑΙ ΣΕ ΤΟ ΣΟΝ ΑΥΘΕΝΤΙΚΟΝ ΣΟΥ ΟΝΟΜΑ ΕΝ ΟΙΣ ΟΥ ΔΥΝΗ ΠΑΡΑΚΟΥΣΑΙ ΙΩΕΡΒΗΘ, ΙΩΠΑΚΕΡΒΗΟ, ΙΩΒΟΛΧΩΣΗΘ, ΙΩΠΑΤΑΘΝΑΖ, ΙΩΣΩΡΩ, ΙΩΝΕΒΟΥΤΟΣΟΥΑΛΗΘ, ΑΚΤΙΩΦΙ, ΕΡΕΣΧΙΓΑΛ, ΝΕΒΟΠΟΩΑΛΗΘ, ΑΒΕΡΑΜΕΝΘΩΟΝ, ΛΕΡΘΕΞΑΝΑΞ, ΕΘΡΕΛΥΩΘ, ΝΕΜΑΡΕΒΑ, ΑΕΜΙΝΑ, ΟΛΟΝ ΗΚΕ ΜΟΙ ΚΑΙ ΒΑΔΙΣΟΝ ΚΑΙ ΚΑΤΕΒΑΛΕ ΤΟΝ ΔΕΙΝΟΝ ΜΑΘΕΡΣ. ΡΙΓΕΙ ΚΑΙ ΠΥΡΕΙΩ ΑΥΤΟΣ ΗΔΙΚΗΣΕΝ ΤΟΝ ΑΝΘΩΠΟΝ ΚΑΙ ΤΟ ΑΙΜΑ ΤΟΥ ΦΥΩΝΟΣ ΕΣΚΕΧΥΣΕΝ ΠΑΡ'ΕΑΥΤΩ.

ΔΙΑ ΤΟΥΤΟ ΤΑΥΤΑ ΠΟΙΕΩ ΚΟΙΝΑ.

English Translation

I call upon you, who dwells in the empty spirit—
dreadful, invisible, all-sovereign,
God of gods, the bringer of ruin, and maker of omens,
the one who hates a house made steadfast,
for you were vomited out of Egypt and cast into the outer lands.
You were named the all-testing one,
and the one who cannot be overcome.
I call upon you—Typhon-Seth— to fulfill your oracles,
for I invoke your true and sovereign name,
by which you cannot ignore me:
Io-Erbēth, Io-Pakerbiō, Io-Bolchōsēth, Io-Patathnaz,
Io-Sōrō, Io-Neboutosoualēth, Aktiōphi, Ereschigal,
Nebopoōalēth, Aberamenthōon, Lerthēxanax, Ethrelyōth,
Nemareba, Aemina, Holon—
Come to me, walk, and cast down the Dread One, Magez.
He shook, and with fire he wronged mankind,
and the blood of the race was poured out by his own hand.
For this reason, I make these things common.

Notes:

"Typhon-Seth": Typhon (Greek chaos-monster) and Seth (Egyptian god of chaos and deserts) were syncretized in late Hellenistic and magical texts as powers opposed to divine order.

"Maker of omens" (ἐπημοποιόν) and "bringer of ruin" (φθεροποιόν) indicate destructive cosmic functions—used not with hatred, but reverence and fear.

"Cannot be overcome" (μὴ νικώμενος): a classic epithet of deities in magical papyri.

The name-list includes many voces magicae—words of power with no direct translation, meant to carry vibrational or spiritual significance.

"Magez" is unclear—it may be a corruption of magus or magoi or simply a spirit's name.

"I make these things common" (ταῦτα ποιῶ κοινά) implies the dissolution of division—communal sharing of power, wisdom, or consequence. Possibly a nod to Gnostic or early Christian egalitarianism.

Preface.

This translation of the FIRST BOOK of the "*Lemegeton*" which is now for the first time made accessible to students of TALISMANIC MAGIC was done, after careful collation and edition, from numerous *Ancient Manuscripts* in *Hebrew, Latin,* and *French,* by G. H. *Fra.* D.D.C.F., by the order of the *Secret Chief* of the *Rosicrucian Order.** The G. H. *Fra.*, having succumbed unhappily to the assaults of the *Four Great Princes* (acting notably under Martial influences), it seemed expedient that the work should be brought to its conclusion by another hand. The investigation of a competent Skryer into the house of our unhappy *Fra.*, confirmed this divination; neither our *Fra.* nor his *Hermetic Mul.* were there seen; but only the terrible shapes of the evil *Adepts* S.V.A.† and H., whose original bodies having

---

*Mr. A. E. Waite writes ("*Real History Of The Rosicrucians,*" p. 426): "I beg leave to warn my readers that all persons who proclaim themselves to be *Rosicrucians* are simply members of pseudo-fraternities, and that there is that difference between their assertion and the fact of the case in which the essence of a lie consists!" It is within the *Editor's* personal knowledge that Mr. Waite was (and still is probably) a member of a society claiming to be the R.C. fraternity As *Mr. Waite* constantly hints in his writing that he is in touch with initiated centres, I think the *syllogism,* whose premises are given above, is fair, if not quite formal.—ED.

†It was owing to our *Fra.* receiving this S.V.A. as his Superior, and giving up the *Arcana* of our *Fraternity* into so unhallowed a power, that We decided no longer to leave Our dignity and authority in the hands of one who could be thus easily imposed upon. (For by a childish and easy magical trick did S.V.A. persuade D.D.C.F. of that lie.)

been sequestered by Justice, were no longer of use to them. On this we stayed no longer Our Hand; but withdrawing Ourselves, and consulting the Rota, and the Books M. and Q. did decide to ask Mr. Aleister Crowley, a poet, and skilled student of *Magical Lore,* and an expert *Kabbalist,* to complete openly that which had been begun in secret.‡ This is that which is written: "His Bishoprick let another take." And again: "*Oculi Tetragammaton.*" This is also that which is said: "Nomen Secundum refertur ad *Gebhurah;* qui est *Rex Bittul* atque Corruptio *Achurajim Patris et Matris* hoc indigitatur."

And so saying we wish you well.

Ex Deo Nascimur.
In Jesu Morimur.
Per S.S. Reviviscimus.

Given forth from our Mountain of A.,
   this day of C.C. 1903 A. D.

‡He that is appointed to complete in secret that which had been begun openly is R.R., and to be heard of at the care of the Editor.

PRELIMINARY INVOCATION.

Thee I invoke, the Bornless one.
Thee, that didst create the Earth and the Heavens:
Thee, that didst create the Night and the Day.
Thee, that didst create the Darkness and the Light.
Thou art Osorronophris: Whom no man has seen at any time.
Thou art Jäbas
Thou art Jäpōs:
Thou hast distinguished between the Just and the Unjust.
Thou didst make the Female and the Male.
Thou didst produce the Seed and the Fruit.
Thou didst form Men to love one another, and to hate one another.

I am Mosheh Thy Prophet, unto Whom Thou didst commit Thy Mysteries, the Ceremonies of Ishrael:
Thou didst produce the moist and the dry, and that which nourisheth all created Life.
Hear Thou Me, for I am the Angel of Paphrō Osorronophris: this is Thy True Name, handed down to the Prophets of Ishrael.

* * * *

Hear Me:—
Ar: Thiao: Rheibet: Atheleberseth:
A: Blatha: Abeu: Ebeu: Phi:
Thitasoe: Ib: Thiao.

Hear Me, and make all Spirits subject unto Me: so that every Spirit of the Firmament and of the Ether; upon the Earth and under the Earth: on dry Land and in the Water: of Whirling Air, and of rushing Fire: and every Spell and Scourge of God may be obedient unto Me.

****

I invoke Thee, the Terrible and Invisible God: Who dwellest in the Void Place of the Spirit:—
Arogogorobraō: Sothou:
Modoriō: Phalarthaō: Döö: Apé, The Bornless One:
Hear Me: etc.

****

Hear me:—
Roubriaō: Mariōdam: Balbnabaoth: Assalonai: Aphniaō: I: Thoteth: Abrasar: Aëöōü: Ischure, Mighty and Bornless One!
Hear me: etc.

****

I invoke thee:—
  Ma: Barraiō: Jōēl: Kotha:
  Athorēbalō: Abraoth:
Hear Me: etc.

****

Hear me!
Aōth: Abaōth: Basum: Isak:
Sabaoth: Iao:

This is the Lord of the Gods:
This is the Lord of the Universe:
This is He Whom the Winds fear.

This is He, Who having made Voice by His Commandment, is Lord of All Things; King, Ruler and Helper.

Hear Me, etc.

Hear Me:—
Ieou: Pūr: Iou: Pūr: Iaōt: Iaeō: Ioou: Abrasar: Sabriam: Do: Uu: Adonaie: Ede: Edu: Angelos ton Theon: Aniaia Lai: Gaia: Ape: Diathanna Thorun.

I am He! the Bornless Spirit! having sight in the feet: Strong, and the Immortal Fire!
I am He! the Truth!
I am He! Who hate that evil should be wrought in the World!
I am He, that lighteneth and thundereth.
I am He, from Whom is the Shower of the Life of Earth:
I am He, Whose mouth ever flameth:
I am He, the Begetter and Manifester unto the Light:
I am He; the Grace of the World:

"The Heart Girt with a Serpent" is My Name!

Come Thou forth, and follow Me: and make all Spirits subject unto Me so that every Spirit of the Firmament, and of the Ether: upon the Earth and under the Earth: on dry Land, or in the Water: of whirling Air or of rushing Fire: and every Spell and Scourge of God, may be obedient unto me!

Iao: Sabao:

Such are the Words!

Goetia

The Lesser Key Of Solomon

THE INITIATED INTERPRETATION OF CEREMONIAL MAGIC.

It is loftily amusing to the student of *Magical* literature who is not quite a fool—and rare is such a combination!—to note the criticism directed by the Philistine against the citadel of his science. Truly, since our childhood has ingrained into us not only literal belief in the Bible, but also substantial belief in *Alf Laylah* wa *Laylah,* and only adolescence can cure us, we are only too liable, in the rush and energy of dawning manhood, to overturn roughly and rashly both these classics, to regard them both on the same level, as interesting documents from the standpoint of folk-lore and anthropology, and as nothing more.

Even when we learn that the Bible, by a profound and minute study of the text, may be forced to yield up *Qabalistic* arcana of cosmic scope and importance, we are too often slow to apply a similar restorative to the companion volume, even if we are the luck holders of Burton's veritable edition.

To me, then, it remains to raise the *Alf Laylah* wa Laylah into its proper place once more.

I am not concerned to deny the objective reality of all *"magical"* phenomena; if they are illusions, they are at least as real as many unquestioned facts of daily life; and, if we follow Herbert Spencer, they are at least evidence of some cause.[1]

Now, this fact is our base. What is the cause of my illusion of seeing a spirit in the triangle of Art?

Every smatterer, every expert in psychology, will answer: "That cause lies in your brain."

English children (*pace* the Education Act) are taught that the Universe lies in infinite Space; Hindu children, in the Akasa, which is the same thing.

Those Europeans who go a little deeper learn from Fichte, that the phenomenal Universe is the creation of the Ego; Hindus, or Europeans studying under Hindu Gurus, are told, that by Akasa is meant the Chitakasa. The Chitakasa is situated in the "Third Eye," *i.e.*, in the brain. By assuming higher dimensions of space, we can assimilate this fact to Realism; but we have no need to take so much trouble.

This being true for the ordinary Universe, that all sense-impressions are dependent on changes in the brain,[2] we must include illusions, which are after all sense-impressions as much as "realities" are, in the class of "phenomena dependent on brain-changes."

Magical phenomena, however, come under a special sub-class, since they are willed, and their cause is the series of "real" phenomena called the operations of ceremonial Magic.

[1] This, incidentally, is perhaps the greatest argument we possess, pushed to its extreme, against the Advaitist theories.
[2] Thought is a secretion of the brain (Weissmann). Consciousness is a function of the brain (Huxley).

THE LESSER KEY

These consist of
- (1) Sight.
    The circle, square, triangle, vessels, lamps, robes, implements, etc.
- (2) Sound.
    The invocations.
- (3) Smell.
    The perfumes.
- (4) Taste.
    The Sacraments.
- (5) Touch.
    As under (1).
- (6) Mind.
    The combination of all these and reflection on their significance.

These unusual impressions (1-5) produce unusual brain-changes; hence their summary (6) is of unusual kind. Its projection back into the apparently phenomenal world is therefore unusual.

Herein then consists the reality of the operations and effects of ceremonial magic,[1] and I conceive that the apology is ample, as far as the "effects" refer only to those phenomena which appear to the magician himself, the appearance of the spirit, his conversation, possible shocks from imprudence, and so on, even to ecstasy on the one hand, and death or madness on the other.

But can any of the effects described in this our book Goetia be obtained, and if so, can you give a rational explanation of the circumstances? Say you so?

I can, and will.

The spirits of the Goetia are portions of the human brain.

[1] Apart from its value in obtaining one-pointedness.

Their seals therefore represent (Mr. Spencer's projected cube) methods of stimulating or regulating those particular spots (through the eye).

The names of God are vibrations calculated to establish:

(*a*) General control of the brain. (Establishment of functions relative to the subtle world.)

(*b*) Control over the brain in detail. (Rank or type of the Spirit.)

(*c*) Control of one special portion. (Name of the Spirit.)

The perfumes aid this through smell. Usually the perfume will only tend to control a large area; but there is an attribution of perfumes to letters of the alphabet enabling one, by a Qabalistic formula, to spell out the Spirit's name.

I need not enter into more particular discussion of these points; the intelligent reader can easily fill in what is lacking.

If, then, I say, with Solomon:

"The Spirit Cimieries teaches logic," what I mean is:

"Those portions of my brain which subserve the logical faculty may be stimulated and developed by following out the processes called 'The Invocation of Cimieries.'"

And this is a purely materialistic rational statement; it is independent of any objective hierarchy at all. Philosophy has nothing to say; and Science can only suspend judgment, pending a proper and methodical investigation of the facts alleged.

Unfortunately, we cannot stop there. Solomon promises us that we can (1) obtain information; (2) destroy our enemies; (3) understand the voices of nature; (4) obtain treasure; (5) heal diseases, etc. I have taken

THE LESSER KEY

these five powers at random; considerations of space forbid me to explain all.

(1) Brings up facts from sub-consciousness.

(2) Here we come to an interesting fact. It is curious to note the contrast between the noble means and the apparently vile ends of magical rituals. The latter are disguises for sublime truths. "To destroy our enemies" is to realize the illusion of duality, to excite compassion.

(Ah! Mr. Waite, the world of Magic is a mirror, wherein who sees muck is muck.)

(3) A careful naturalist will understand much from the voices of the animals he has studied long. Even a child knows the difference of a cat's miauling and purring. The faculty may be greatly developed.

(4) Business capacity may be stimulated.

(5) Abnormal states of the body may be corrected, and the involved tissues brought back to tone, in obedience to currents started from the brain.

So for all other phenomena. There is no effect which is truly and necessarily miraculous.

Our Ceremonial Magic fines down, then, to a series of minute, though of course empirical, physiological experiments, and whoso will carry them through intelligently need not fear the result.

I have all the health, and treasure, and logic, I need; I have no time to waste. "There is a lion in the way." For me these practices are useless; but for the benefit of others less fortunate I give them to the world, together with this explanation of, and apology for, them.

I trust that the explanation will enable many students who have hitherto, by a puerile objectivity in their view of the question, obtained no results, to succeed; that the apology may impress upon our scornful men of science that the study of the bacillus should give place to that of the baculum, the little to the great—how great one only realizes when one identifies the wand with the Mahalingam, up which Brahma flew at the rate of 84,000 yojanas a second for 84,000 mahakalpas, down which Vishnu flew at the rate of 84,000 croces of yojanas a second for 84,000 crores of mahakalpas—yet neither reached an end.

But I reach an end.

Boleskine House,
   Foyers, N.B.

PRELIMINARY DEFINITION OF MAGIC.

LEMEGETON VEL CLAVICULA SALOMONIS REGIS.

MAGIC is the Highest, most Absolute, and most Divine Knowledge of Natural Philosophy,[1] advanced in its works and wonderful operations by a right understanding of the inward and occult virtue of things; so that true Agents[2] being applied to proper Patients,[3] strange and admirable effects will thereby be produced. Whence magicians are profound and diligent searchers into Nature; they, because of their skill, know how to anticipate an effort,[4] the which to the vulgar shall seem to be a miracle.

Origen saith that the Magical Art doth not contain anything subsisting, but although it should, yet that it must not be Evil, or subject to contempt or scorn; and doth distinguish the *Natural Magic* from that which is *Diabolical*.

Apollonius Tyannaeus only exercised the *Natural Magic*, by the which he did perform wonderful things.

Philo Hebraeus saith that true Magic, by which we do arrive at the understanding of the Secret Works of Nature, is so far from being contemptible that the greatest Monarchs and Kings have studied it. Nay! among the Persians none might reign unless he was skilful in this GREAT ART.

[1] This Preliminary Definition of Magic is found in very few Codices, and is probably later than the body of the work.
[2] Or Actives.
[3] Or Passives.
[4] Or Effect.

This Noble Science often degenerateth, from *Natural* becometh *Diabolical*, and from *True Philosophy* turneth unto *Nigromancy*.[1] The which is wholly to be charged upon its followers, who, abusing or not being capable of that High and Mystical Knowledge do immediately hearken unto the temptations of *Sathan*, and are misled by him into the Study of the *Black Art*. Hence it is that Magic lieth under disgrace, and they who seek after it are vulgarly esteemed *Sorcerers*.

The Fraternity of the Rosie Crusians thought it not fit to style themselves Magicians, but rather Philosophers. And they be not ignorant Empiricks,[2] but learned and experienced Physicians, whose remedies be not only *Lawful* but *Divine*.

THE BRIEF INTRODUCTORY DESCRIPTION.

(N.B. This is taken from several MS. Codices, of which the four principal variations are here composed together in parallel columns as an example of the close agreement of the various texts of the Lemegeton.

For in the whole work the differences in the wording of the various Codices are not sufficient to require the constant giving of parallel readings; but except in the more ancient examples there is much deterioration in the Seals and Sigils, so that in this latter respect the more recent exemplars are not entirely reliable.)

CLAVICULA SALOMONIS REGIS,

which containeth all the Names, Offices, and Orders of all the Spirits that ever he had converse with, with the

---

[1] Or the Black Art, as distinct from mere Necromancy, or Divination by the Dead.

[2] Or Quacks and Pretenders. Vide note on p. 10.

Seals and Characters to each Spirit and the manner of calling them forth to visible appearance:

In 5 parts, viz.:

(1) THE FIRST PART is a Book of Evil Spirits, called GOETIA, showing how he bound up those Spirits, and used them in general things, whereby he obtained great fame.

(2) THE SECOND PART is a Book of Spirits, partly Evil and partly Good, which is named THEURGIA-GOETIA, all Aërial Spirits, etc.

(3) THE THIRD PART is of Spirits governing the Planetary Hours, and what Spirits belong to every degree, of the Signs, and Planets in the Signs. Called the PAULINE ART, etc.

(4) THE FOURTH PART of this Book is called ALMADEL or SOLOMON, which containeth those Spirits which govern the Four Altitudes, or the 360 Degrees of the Zodiac.

These two last Orders of Spirits are Good, and to be sought for by Divine seeking, etc., and are called THEURGIA.

(5) THE FIFTH PART is a Book of Orations and Prayers that Wise Solomon used upon the Altar in the Temple. The which is called ARS NOVA, which was revealed unto Solomon by that Holy Angel of God called MICHAEL; and he also received many brief Notes written with the Finger of God, which were declared to him by the said Angel with Claps of Thunder; without which Notes King Solomon had never obtained his great knowledge, for by them in a short time he knew all Arts and Sciences both Good and Bad; from these Notes it is called the NOTARY ART, etc.

The Whole Lemegeton or Clavicula.

Now this Book containeth all the Names, Orders, and Offices of all the Spirits with which Solomon ever conversed, the Seals and Characters belonging to each Spirit, and the manner of calling them forth to visible appearance:

Divided into 5 special Books or parts, viz.:

(1) The First Book, or Part, which is a Book concerning Spirits of Evil, and which is termed The Goetia of Solomon, sheweth forth his manner of binding these Spirits for use in things divers. And hereby did he acquire great renown.

(2) The Second Book is one which treateth of Spirits mingled of Good and Evil Natures, the which is entitled The Theurgia-Goetia, or the Magical Wisdom of the Spirits Aërial, whereof some do abide, but certain do wander and abide not.

(3) The Third Book, called Ars Paulina, or The Art Pauline, treateth of the Spirits allotted unto every degree of the 360 Degrees of the Zodiac; and also of the Signs, and of the Planets in the Signs, as well as of the Hours.

(4) The Fourth Book, called Ars Almadel Salomonis, or The Art Almadel of Solomon, concerneth those Spirits which be set over the Quaternary of the Altitudes.

These two last mentioned Books, the Art Pauline and the Art Almadel, do relate unto Good Spirits alone, whose knowledge is to be obtained through seeking unto the Divine. These two Books be also classed together under the Name of the First and Second Parts of the Book Theurgia of Solomon.

(5) The Fifth Book of the Lemegeton is one of

Prayers and Orations. The which Solomon the Wise did use upon the Altar in the Temple. And the titles hereof be ARS NOVA, the NEW ART, and ARS NOTARIA, the NOTARY ART. The which was revealed to him by MICHAEL, that Holy Angel of God, in thunder and in lightning, and he further did receive by the aforesaid Angel certain Notes written by the Hand of God, without the which that Great King had never attained unto his great Wisdom, for thus he knew all things and all Sciences and Arts whether Good or Evil.

CLAVICULA SALOMONIS REGIS,

which containeth all the Names, Offices, and Orders of all the Spirits with whom he ever held any converse; together with the Seals and Characters proper unto each Spirit, and the method of calling them forth to visible appearance:

In 5 parts, viz.:

(1) THE FIRST PART is a Book of Evil Spirits, called GOETIA, showing how he bound up those Spirits and used them in things general and several, whereby he obtained great fame.

(2) THE SECOND PART is a Book of Spirits, partly Evil and partly Good, which is called THEURGIA-GOETIA, all Aërial Spirits, etc.

(3) THE THIRD PART is of Spirits governing the Planetary Hours, and of what Spirits do belong to every Degree of the Signs, and of the Planets in the Signs. This is called the PAULINE ART, etc.

(4) THE FOURTH PART of this Book is called ALMADEL OF SOLOMON, the which containeth those Spirits which do govern the Four Altitudes, or the 360 Degrees of the Zodiac.

These two last Orders of Spirits are Good, and are

called THEURGIA, and are to be sought for by Divine seeking, etc.

(5) THE FIFTH PART is a Book of Orations and Prayers which Wise Solomon did use upon the Altar in the Temple. The which is called ARS NOVA, the which was revealed to Solomon by that Holy Angel of God called Michael; and he also received many brief Notes written with the Finger of God, which were declared to him by the said Angel with Claps of Thunder; without which Notes King Solomon had never obtained his Great Wisdom, for by them in short time he gained Knowledge of all Arts and Sciences both Good and Bad; from these Notes it is called the NOTARY ART, etc.

THE BOOK OF EVIL SPIRITS.

THE KEY OF SOLOMON, which contains all the names, orders, and offices of all the Spirits that ever Solomon conversed with, together with the Seals and Characters belonging to each Spirit, and the manner of calling them forth to visible appearance:

In 4 parts.

(1) THE FIRST PART is a Book of Evil Spirits, called GOETIA, showing how he bound up those Spirits and used them in several things, whereby he obtained great fame.

(2) THE SECOND PART is a Book of Spirits, partly Good and partly Evil, which is named THEURGIA-GOETIA, all Aërial Spirits, etc.

(3) THE THIRD PART is a Book governing the Planetary Houses, and what Spirits belong to every Degree of the Signs, and Planets in the Signs. Called the Pauline Art.

(4) THE FOURTH PART is a Book called the ALMADEL OF SOLOMON, which contains Twenty Chief Spirits who govern the Four Altitudes, or the 360 Degrees of the Zodiac.

These two last Orders of Spirits are Good, and called THEURGIA, and are to be sought after by Divine seeking.

These Most Sacred Mysteries were revealed unto Solomon.

Now in this Book LEMEGETON is contained the whole Art of King Solomon. And although there be many other Books that are said to be his, yet none is to be compared hereunto, for this containeth them all. Though there be titles with several other Names of the Book, as THE BOOK HELISOL, which is the very same with this last Book of Lemegeton called ARS NOVA or ARS NOTARIA, etc.

These Books were first found in the Chaldee and Hebrew Tongues at Jerusalem by a Jewish Rabbi; and by him put into the Greek language and thence into the Latin, as it is said.

SHEMHAMPHORASH.

(1.) BAEL.—The First Principal Spirit is a King ruling in the East, called Bael. He maketh thee to go Invisible. He ruleth over 66 Legions of Infernal Spirits. He appeareth in divers shapes, sometimes like a Cat, sometimes like a Toad, and sometimes like a Man, and sometimes all these forms at once. He speaketh hoarsely. This is his character which is used to be worn as a Lamen before him who calleth him forth, or else he will not do thee homage.

(2.) AGARES.—The Second Spirit is a Duke called Agreas, or Agares. He is under the Power of the East, and cometh up in the form of an old fair Man, riding upon a Crocodile, carrying a Goshawk upon his fist, and yet mild in appearance. He maketh them to run that stand still, and bringeth back runaways. He teaches all Languages or Tongues presently. He hath power also to destroy Dignities both Spiritual and Temporal, and causeth Earthquakes. He was of the Order of Virtues. He hath under his government 31 Legions of Spirits. And this is his Seal or Character which thou shalt wear as a Lamen before thee.

(3.) VASSAGO.—The Third Spirit is a Mighty Prince, being of the same nature as Agares. He is called Vassago. This Spirit is of a Good Nature, and his office is to declare things Past and to Come, and to discover all things Hid or Lost. And he governeth 26 Legions of Spirits, and this is his Seal.

(4.) SAMIGINA, or GAMIGIN.—The Fourth Spirit is Samigina, a Great Marquis. He appeareth in the form of a little Horse or Ass, and then into Human shape doth he change himself at the request of the Master. He speaketh with a hoarse voice. He ruleth over 30 Legions of Inferiors. He teaches all Liberal Sciences, and giveth account of Dead Souls that died in sin. And his Seal is this, which is to be worn before the Magician when he is Invocator, etc.

(5.) MARBAS.—The fifth Spirit is Marbas. He is a Great President, and appeareth at first in the form of a Great Lion, but afterwards, at the request of the Master, he putteth on Human Shape. He answereth truly of things Hidden or Secret. He causeth Diseases and cureth them. Again, he giveth great Wisdom and Knowledge in Mechanical Arts; and can change men into other shapes. He governeth 36 Legions of Spirits. And his Seal is this, which is to be worn as aforesaid.

(6.) VALEFOR.—The Sixth Spirit is Valefor. He is a mighty Duke, and appeareth in the shape of a Lion with an Ass's Head, bellowing. He is a good Familiar, but tempteth them he is a familiar of to steal. He governeth 10 Legions of Spirits. His Seal is this, which is to be worn, whether thou wilt have him for a Familiar, or not.

(7.) AMON.—The Seventh Spirit is Amon. He is a Marquis great in power, and most stern. He appeareth like a Wolf with a Serpent's tail, vomiting out of his mouth flames of fire; but at the command of the Magician he putteth on the shape of a Man with Dog's teeth beset in a head like a Raven; or else like a Man with a Raven's head (simply). He telleth all things Past and to Come. He procureth feuds and reconcileth controversies between friends. He governeth 40 Legions of Spirits. His Seal is this which is to be worn as aforesaid, etc.

(8.) BARBATOS.—The Eighth Spirit is Barbatos. He is a Great Duke, and appeareth when the Sun is in Sagittary, with four noble Kings and their companies of great troops. He giveth understanding of the singing of Birds, and of the Voices of other creatures, such as the barking of Dogs. He breaketh the Hidden Treasures open that have been laid by the Enchantments of Magicians. He is of the Order of Virtues, of which some part he retaineth still; and he knoweth all things Past, and to come, and conciliateth Friends and those that be in Power. He ruleth over 30 Legions of Spirits. His Seal of Obedience is this, the which wear before thee as aforesaid.

(9) PAIMON.—The Ninth Spirit in this Order is Paimon, a Great King, and very obedient unto LUCIFER. He appeareth in the form of a Man sitting upon a Dromedary with a Crown most glorious upon his head. There goeth before him also an Host of Spirits, like Men with Trumpets and well sounding Cymbals, and all other sorts of Musical Instruments. He hath a great Voice, and roareth at his first coming, and his speech is such that the Magician cannot well understand unless he can compel him. This Spirit can teach all Arts and Sciences, and other secret things. He can discover unto thee what the Earth is, and what holdeth it up in the Waters; and what Mind is, and where it is; or any other thing thou mayest desire to know. He giveth Dignity, and confirmeth the same. He bindeth or maketh any man subject unto the Magician if he so desire it. He giveth good Familiars, and such as can teach all Arts. He is to be observed towards the West. He is of the Order of Dominations.[1] He hath under him 200 Legions of Spirits, and part of them are of the Order of Angels, and the other part of Potentates. Now if thou callest this Spirit Paimon alone, thou must make him some offering; and

[1] Or Dominions, as they are usually termed.

there will attend him two Kings called Labal and Abalim, and also other Spirits who be of the Order of Potentates in his Host, and 25 Legions. And those Spirits which be subject unto them are not always with them unless the Magician do compel them. His Character is this which must be worn as a Lamen before thee, etc.

(10.) Buer.—The Tenth Spirit is Buer, a Great President. He appeareth in Sagittary, and that is his shape when the Sun is there. He teaches Philosophy, both Moral and Natural, and the Logic Art, and also the Virtues of all Herbs and Plants. He healeth all distempers in man, and giveth good Familiars. He governeth 50 Legions of Spirits, and his Character of obedience is this, which thou must wear when thou callest him forth unto appearance.

(11.) Gusion.—The Eleventh Spirit in order is a great and strong Duke, called Gusion. He appeareth like a Xenopilus. He telleth all things, Past, Present, and to Come, and showeth the meaning and resolution of all questions thou mayest ask. He conciliateth and reconcileth friendships, and giveth Honour and Dignity unto any. He ruleth over 40 Legions of Spirits. His Seal is this, the which wear thou as aforesaid.

(12.) Sitri.—The Twelfth Spirit is Sitri. He is a Great Prince and appeareth at first with a Leopard's head and the Wings of a Gryphon, but after the command of the Master of the Exorcism he putteth on Human shape, and that very beautiful. He enflameth men with Women's love, and Women with Men's love; and causeth them also to show themselves naked if it be desired. He governeth 60 Legions of Spirits. His Seal is this, to be worn as a Lamen before thee, etc.

(13.) Beleth.—The Thirteenth Spirit is called Beleth

(or Bileth, or Bilet). He is a mighty King and terrible. He rideth on a pale horse with trumpets and other kinds of musical instruments playing before him. He is very furious at his first appearance, that is, while the Exorcist layeth his courage; for to do this he must hold a Hazel Wand in his hand, striking it out towards the South and East Quarters, make a triangle, △, without the Circle, and then command him into it by the Bonds and Charges of Spirits as hereafter followeth. And if he doth not enter into the triangle, △, at your threats, rehearse the Bonds and Charms before him, and then he will yield Obedience and come into it, and do what he is commanded by the Exorcist. Yet he must receive him courteously because he is a Great King, and do homage unto him, as the Kings and Princes do that attend upon him. And thou must have always a Silver Ring on the middle finger of the left hand held against thy face,[1] as they do yet before AMAYMON. This Great King Beleth causeth all the love that may be, both of Men and of Women, until the Master Exorcist hath had his desire fulfilled. He is of the Order of Powers, and he governeth 85 Legions of Spirits. His Noble Seal is this, which is to be worn before thee at working.

(14.) LERAJE, or LERAIKHA.—The Fourteenth Spirit is called Leraje (or Leraie). He is a Marquis Great in Power, showing himself in the likeness of an Archer clad in Green, and carrying a Bow and Quiver. He causeth all great Battles and Contests; and maketh wounds to putrefy that are made with Arrows by Archers. This belongeth unto Sagittary. He governeth 30 Legions of Spirits, and this is his Seal, etc.

---

[1] To protect him from the flaming breath of the enraged Spirit; the design is given at the end of the instructions for the Magical Circle, etc., later on in the Goetia.

(15.) ELIGOS.—The Fifteenth Spirit in Order is Eligos, a Great Duke, and appeareth in the form of a goodly Knight, carrying a Lance, an Ensign, and a Serpent. He discovereth hidden things, and knoweth things to come; and of Wars, and how the Soldiers will or shall meet. He causeth the Love of Lords and Great Persons. He governeth 60 Legions of Spirits. His Seal is this, etc.

(16.) ZEPAR.—The Sixteenth Spirit is Zepar. He is a Great Duke, and appeareth in Red Apparel and Armour, like a Soldier. His office is to cause Women to love Men, and to bring them together in love. He also maketh them barren. He governeth 26 Legions of Inferior Spirits, and his Seal is this, which he obeyeth when he seeth it.

(17.) BOTIS.—The Seventeenth Spirit is Botis, a Great President, and an Earl. He appeareth at the first show in the form of an ugly Viper, then at the command of the Magician he putteth on a Human shape with Great Teeth, and two Horns, carrying a bright and sharp Sword in his hand. He telleth all things Past, and to Come, and reconcileth Friends and Foes. He ruleth over 60 Legions of Spirits, and this is his Seal, etc.

(18.) BATHIN.—The Eighteenth Spirit is Bathin. He is a Mighty and Strong Duke, and appeareth like a Strong Man with the tail of a Serpent, sitting upon a Pale-Coloured Horse. He knoweth the Virtues of Herbs and Precious Stones, and can transport men suddenly from one country to another. He ruleth over 30 Legions of Spirits. His Seal is this which is to be worn as aforesaid.

(19.) SALLOS.—The Nineteenth Spirit is Sallos (or Saleos). He is a Great and Mighty Duke, and appeareth in the form of a gallant Soldier riding on a Crocodile, with a Ducal Crown on his head, but peaceably. He causeth the Love of Women to Men, and of Men to Women; and governeth 30 Legions of Spirits. His Seal is this, etc.

(20.) PURSON.—The Twentieth Spirit is Purson, a Great King. His appearance is comely, like a Man with a Lion's face, carrying a cruel Viper in his hand, and riding upon a Bear. Going before him are many Trumpets sounding. He knoweth all things hidden, and can discover Treasure, and tell all things Past, Present, and to Come. He can take a Body either Human or Aërial, and answereth truly of all Earthly things both Secret and Divine, and of the Creation of the World. He bringeth forth good Familiars, and under his Government there be 22 Legions of Spirits, partly of the Order of Virtues and partly of the Order of Thrones. His Mark, Seal, or Character is this, unto the which he oweth obedience, and which thou shalt wear in time of action, etc.

(21.) MARAX.—The Twenty-first Spirit is Marax.[1] He is a Great Earl and President. He appeareth like a great Bull with a Man's face. His office is to make Men very knowing in Astronomy, and all other Liberal Sciences; also he can give good Familiars, and wise, knowing the virtues of Herbs and Stones which be precious. He governeth 30 Legions of Spirits, and his Seal is this, which must be made and worn as aforesaid, etc.

(22.) IPOS.—The Twenty-second Spirit is Ipos. He is an Earl, and a Mighty Prince, and appeareth in the form of an Angel with a Lion's Head, and a Goose's Foot, and Hare's Tail. He knoweth all things Past, Present, and to Come. He maketh men witty and bold.

---

[1] In some Codices written Morax, but I consider the above the correct orthography.

THE LESSER KEY

He governeth 36 Legions of Spirits. His Seal is this, which thou shalt wear, etc.

(23.) AIM.—The Twenty-third Spirit is Aim. He is a Great Strong Duke. He appeareth in the form of a very handsome Man in body, but with three Heads; the first, like a Serpent, the second like a Man having two Stars on his Forehead, the third like a Calf. He rideth on a Viper, carrying a Firebrand in his Hand, wherewith he setteth cities, castles, and great Places, on fire. He maketh thee witty in all manner of ways, and giveth true answers unto private matters. He governeth 26 Legions of Inferior Spirits; and his Seal is this, which wear thou as aforesaid, etc.

(24.) NABERIUS.—The Twenty-fourth Spirit is Naberius. He is a most valiant Marquis, and showeth in the form of a Black Crane, fluttering about the Circle, and when he speaketh it is with a hoarse voice. He maketh men cunning in all Arts and Sciences, but especially in the Art of Rhetoric. He restoreth lost Dignities and Honours. He governeth 19 Legions of Spirits. His Seal is this, which is to be worn, etc.

(25.) GLASYA-LABOLAS.—The Twenty-fifth Spirit is Glasya-Labolas. He is a Mighty President and Earl, and showeth himself in the form of a Dog with Wings like a Gryphon. He teacheth all Arts and Sciences in an instant, and is an Author of Bloodshed and Manslaughter. He teacheth all things Past, and to Come. If desired he causeth the love both of Friends and of Foes. He can make a Man to go Invisible. And he hath under his command 36 Legions of Spirits. His Seal is this, to be, etc.

(26.) BUNE, or BIMÉ.—The Twenty-sixth Spirit is Buné (or Bim). He is a Strong, Great and Mighty Duke. He appeareth in the form of a Dragon with three heads, one like a Dog, one like a Gryphon, and one like a Man. He speaketh with a high and comely Voice. He changeth the Place of the Dead, and causeth the Spirits which be under him to gather together upon your Sepulchres. He giveth Riches unto a Man, and maketh him Wise and Eloquent. He giveth true Answers unto Demands. And he governeth 30 Legions of Spirits. His Seal is this, unto the which he oweth Obedience. He hath another Seal (which is the first of these,[1] but the last is the best).[2]

(27.) RONOVÉ.—The Twenty-seventh Spirit is Ronové. He appeareth in the Form of a Monster. He teacheth the Art of Rhetoric very well and giveth Good Servants, Knowledge of Tongues, and Favours with Friends or Foes. He is a Marquis and Great Earl; and there be under his command 19 Legions of Spirits. His Seal is this, etc.

(28.) BERITH.—The Twenty-eighth Spirit in Order, as Solomon bound them, is named Berith. He is a Mighty, Great, and Terrible Duke. He hath two other Names given unto him by men of later times, viz.: BEALE, or BEAL, and BOFRY or BOLFRY. He appeareth in the Form of a Soldier with Red Clothing, riding upon a Red Horse, and having a Crown of Gold upon his head. He giveth true answers, Past, Present, and to Come. Thou must make use of a Ring in calling him forth, as is before spoken of regarding Beleth.[3] He can turn all metals into Gold. He can give Dignities, and can confirm them unto Man. He speaketh with a very clear and subtle Voice. He governeth 26 Legions of Spirits. His Seal is this, etc.

(29.) ASTAROTH.—The Twenty-ninth Spirit is Astaroth. He is a Mighty, Strong Duke, and appeareth in

---

[1] Figure 30.   [2] Figure 31.   [3] See *ante*, Spirit No. 13.

the Form of an hurtful Angel riding on an Infernal Beast like a Dragon, and carrying in his right hand a Viper. Thou must in no wise let him approach too near unto thee, lest he do thee damage by his Noisome Breath. Wherefore the Magician must hold the Magical Ring near his face, and that will defend him. He giveth true answers of things Past, Present, and to Come, and can discover all Secrets. He will declare wittingly how the Spirits fell, if desired, and the reason of his own fall. He can make men wonderfully knowing in all Liberal Sciences. He ruleth 40 Legions of Spirits. His Seal is this, which wear thou as a Lamen before thee, or else he will not appear nor yet obey thee, etc.

(30.) FORNEUS.—The Thirtieth Spirit is Forneus. He is a Mighty and Great Marquis, and appeareth in the Form of a Great Sea-Monster. He teacheth, and maketh men wonderfully knowing in the Art of Rhetoric. He causeth men to have a Good Name, and to have the knowledge and understanding of Tongues. He maketh one to be beloved of his Foes as well as of his Friends. He governeth 29 Legions of Spirits, partly of the Order of Thrones, and partly of that of Angels. His Seal is this, which wear thou, etc.

(31.) FORAS.—The Thirty-first Spirit is Foras. He is a Mighty President, and appeareth in the Form of a Strong Man in Human Shape. He can give the understanding to Men how they may know the Virtues of all Herbs and Precious Stones. He teacheth the Arts of Logic and Ethics in all their parts. If desired he maketh men invisible,[1] and to live long, and to be eloquent. He

---

[1] One or two Codices have "invincible," but "invisible" is given in the majority. Yet the form of appearance of Foras as a strong man might warrant the former, though from the nature of his offices the invincibility would probably be rather on the mental than on the physical plane.

can discover Treasures and recover things Lost. He ruleth over 29 Legions of Spirits, and his Seal is this, which wear thou, etc.

(32.) Asmoday.—The Thirty-second Spirit is Asmoday, or Asmodai. He is a Great King, Strong, and Powerful. He appeareth with Three Heads, whereof the first is like a Bull, the second like a Man, and the third like a Ram; he hath also the tail of a Serpent, and from his mouth issue Flames of Fire. His Feet are webbed like those of a Goose. He sitteth upon an Infernal Dragon, and beareth in his hand a Lance with a Banner. He is first and choicest under the Power of Amaymon, he goeth before all other. When the Exorcist hath a mind to call him, let it be abroad, and let him stand on his feet all the time of action, with his Cap or Head-dress off; for if it be on, Amaymon will deceive him and call all his actions to be bewrayed. But as soon as the Exorcist seeth Asmoday in the shape aforesaid, he shall call him by his Name, saying: "Art thou Asmoday?" and he will not deny it, and by-and-by he will bow down unto the ground. He giveth the Ring of Virtues; he teacheth the Arts of Arithmetic, Astronomy, Geometry, and all handicrafts absolutely. He giveth true and full answers unto thy demands. He maketh one Invincible. He showeth the place where Treasures lie, and guardeth it. He, amongst the Legions of Amaymon governeth 72 Legions of Spirits Inferior. His Seal is this which thou must wear as a Lamen upon thy breast, etc.

(33.) Gaap.—The Thirty-third Spirit is Gäap. He is a Great President and a Mighty Prince. He appeareth when the Sun is in some of the Southern Signs, in a Human Shape, going before Four Great and Mighty Kings, as if he were a Guide to conduct them along on their way. His Office is to make men Insensible or

Ignorant; as also in Philosophy to make them Knowing, and in all the Liberal Sciences. He can cause Love or Hatred, also he can teach thee to consecrate those things that belong to the Dominion of AMAYMON his King. He can deliver Familiars out of the Custody of other Magicians, and answereth truly and perfectly of things Past, Present, and to Come. He can carry and re-carry men very speedily from one Kingdom to another, at the Will and Pleasure of the Exorcist. He ruleth over 66 Legions of Spirits, and he was of the Order of Potentates. His Seal is this to be made and to be worn as aforesaid, etc.

(34.) FURFUR.—The Thirty-fourth Spirit is Furfur. He is a Great and Mighty Earl, appearing in the Form of an Hart with a Fiery Tail. He never speaketh truth unless he be compelled, or brought up within a triangle, $\triangle$. Being therein, he will take upon himself the Form of an Angel. Being bidden, he speaketh with a hoarse voice. Also he will wittingly urge Love between Man and Woman. He can raise Lightnings and Thunders, Blasts, and Great Tempestuous Storms. And he giveth True Answers both of Things Secret and Divine, if commanded. He ruleth over 26 Legions of Spirits. And his Seal is this, etc.

(35.) MARCHOSIAS.—The Thirty-fifth Spirit is Marchosias. He is a Great and Mighty Marquis, appearing at first in the Form of a Wolf[1] having Gryphon's Wings, and a Serpent's Tail, and Vomiting Fire out of his mouth. But after a time, at the command of the Exorcist he putteth on the Shape of a Man. And he is a strong fighter. He was of the Order of Dominations. He governeth 30 Legions of Spirits. He told his Chief,

[1] In one Codex of the seventeenth century, very badly written, it might be read "Ox" instead of "Wolf."—TRANS. [For me he appeared always like an ox, and very dazed.—ED.]

who was Solomon, that after 1,200 years he had hopes to return unto the Seventh Throne. And his Seal is this, to be made and worn as a Lamen, etc.

(36.) STOLAS, OR STOLOS.—The Thirty-sixth Spirit is Stolas, or Stolos. He is a Great and Powerful Prince, appearing in the Shape of a Mighty Raven at first before the Exorcist; but after he taketh the image of a Man. He teacheth the Art of Astronomy, and the Virtues of Herbs and Precious Stones. He governeth 26 Legions of Spirits; and his Seal is this, which is, etc.

(37.) PHENEX.—The Thirty-Seventh Spirit is Phenex (or Pheynix). He is a great Marquis, and appeareth like the Bird Phœnix, having the Voice of a Child. He singeth many sweet notes before the Exorcist, which he must not regard, but by-and-by he must bid him put on Human Shape. Then he will speak marvellously of all wonderful Sciences if required. He is a Poet, good and excellent. And he will be willing to perform thy requests. He hath hopes also to return to the Seventh Throne after 1,200 years more, as he said unto Solomon. He governeth 20 Legions of Spirits. And his Seal is this, which wear thou, etc.

(38.) HALPHAS, or MALTHUS.—The Thirty-eighth Spirit is Halphas, or Malthous (or Malthas). He is a Great Earl, and appeareth in the Form of a Stock-Dove. He speaketh with a hoarse Voice. His Office is to build up Towers, and to furnish them with Ammunition and Weapons, and to send Men-of-War[1] to places appointed. He ruleth over 26 Legions of Spirits, and his Seal is this, etc.

(39.) MALPHAS.—The Thirty-ninth Spirit is Malphas. He appeareth at first like a Crow, but after he will put on Human Shape at the request of the Exorcist, and

---

[1] Or Warriors, or Men-at-Arms.

speak with a hoarse Voice. He is a Mighty President and Powerful. He can build Houses and High Towers, and can bring to thy Knowledge Enemies' Desires and Thoughts, and that which they have done. He giveth Good Familiars. If thou makest a Sacrifice unto him he will receive it kindly and willingly, but he will deceive him that doth it. He governeth 40 Legions of Spirits, and his Seal is this, etc.

(40.) RAUM.—The Fortieth Spirit is Räum. He is a Great Earl; and appeareth at first in the Form of a Crow, but after the Command of the Exorcist he putteth on Human Shape. His office is to steal Treasures out King's Houses, and to carry it whither he is commanded, and to destroy Cities and Dignities of Men, and to tell all things, Past, and What Is, and what Will Be; and to cause Love between Friends and Foes. He was of the Order of Thrones. He governeth 30 Legions of Spirits; and his Seal is this, which wear thou as aforesaid.

(41.) FOCALOR.—The Forty-first Spirit is Focalor, or Forcalor, or Furcalor. He is a Mighty Duke and Strong. He appeareth in the Form of a Man with Gryphon's Wings. His office is to slay Men, and to drown them in the Waters, and to overthrow Ships of War, for he hath Power over both Winds and Seas; but he will not hurt any man or thing if he be commanded to the contrary by the Exorcist. He also hath hopes to return to the Seventh Throne after 1,000 years. He governeth 30 Legions of Spirits, and his Seal is this, etc.

(42.) VEPAR.—The Forty-second Spirit is Vepar, or Vephar. He is a Duke Great and Strong and appeareth like a Mermaid. His office is to govern the Waters, and to guide Ships laden with Arms, Armour, and Ammunition, etc., thereon. And at the request of the Exorcist he can cause the seas to be right stormy and to appear full of ships. Also he maketh men to die in Three Days by Putrefying Wounds or Sores, and causing Worms to breed in them. He governeth 29 Legions of Spirits, and his Seal is this, etc.

(43.) SABNOCK.—The Forty-third Spirit, as King Solomon commanded them into the Vessel of Brass, is called Sabnock, or Savnok. He is a Marquis, Mighty, Great and Strong, appearing in the Form of an Armed Soldier with a Lion's Head, riding on a pale-coloured horse. His office is to build high Towers, Castles and Cities, and to furnish them with Armour, etc. Also he can afflict Men for many days with Wounds and with Sores rotten and full of Worms. He giveth Good Familiars at the request of the Exorcist. He commandeth 50 Legions of Spirits; and his Seal is this, etc.

(44.) SHAX.—The Forty-fourth Spirit is Shax, or Shaz (or Shass). He is a Great Marquis and appeareth in the Form of a Stock-Dove, speaking with a voice hoarse, but yet subtle. His Office is to take away the Sight, Hearing, or Understanding of any Man or Woman at the command of the Exorcist; and to steal money out of the houses of Kings, and to carry it again in 1,200 years. If commanded he will fetch Horses at the request of the Exorcist, or any other thing. But he must first be commanded into a Triangle, △, or else he will deceive him, and tell him many Lies. He can discover all things that are Hidden, and not kept by Wicked Spirits. He giveth good Familiars, sometimes. He governeth 30 Legions of Spirits, and his Seal is this, etc.

(45.) VINÉ.—The Forty-fifth Spirit is Viné, or Vinea. He is a Great King, and an Earl; and appeareth in the Form of a Lion,[1] riding upon a Black Horse, and bear-

---

[1] Or "with the Head of a Lion," or "having a Lion's Head," in some Codices.

ing a Viper in his hand. His Office is to discover Things Hidden, Witches, Wizards, and Things Present, Past, and to Come. He, at the command of the Exorcist will build Towers, overthrow Great Stone Walls, and make the Waters rough with Storms. He governeth 36 Legions of Spirits. And his Seal is this, which wear thou, as aforesaid, etc.

(46.) BIFRONS.—The Forty-sixth Spirit is called Bifrons, or Bifröus, or Bifrovs. He is an Earl, and appeareth in the Form of a Monster; but after a while, at the Command of the Exorcist, he putteth on the shape of a Man. His Office is to make one knowing in Astrology, Geometry, and other Arts and Sciences. He teacheth the Virtues of Precious Stones and Woods. He changeth Dead Bodies, and putteth them in another place; also he lighteth seeming Candles upon the Graves of the Dead. He hath under his Command 6 Legions of Spirits. His Seal is this, which he will own and submit unto, etc.

(47.) UVALL, VUAL, or VOVAL.—The Forty-seventh Spirit Uvall, or Vual, or Voval. He is a Duke, Great, Mighty, and Strong; and appeareth in the Form of a Mighty Dromedary at the first, but after a while at the Command of the Exorcist he putteth on Human Shape, and speaketh the Egyptian Tongue, but not perfectly.[1] His Office is to procure the Love of Woman, and to tell Things Past, Present, and to Come. He also procureth Friendship between Friends and Foes. He was of the Order of Potestates or Powers. He governeth 37 Legions of Spirits, and his Seal is this, to be made and worn before thee, etc.

[1] He can nowadays converse in sound though colloquial Coptic.—ED.

(48.) HAAGENTI.—The Forty-eighth Spirit is Haagenti. He is a President, appearing in the Form of a Mighty Bull with Gryphon's Wings. This is at first, but after, at the Command of the Exorcist he putteth on Human Shape. His Office is to make Men wise, and to instruct them in divers things; also to Transmute all Metals into Gold; and to change Wine into Water, and Water into Wine. He governeth 33 Legions of Spirits, and his Seal is this, etc.

(49.) CROCELL.—The Forty-ninth Spirit is Crocell, or Crokel. He appeareth in the Form of an Angel. He is a Duke Great and Strong, speaking something Mystically of Hidden Things. He teacheth the Art of Geometry and the Liberal Sciences. He, at the Command of the Exorcist, will produce Great Noises like the Rushings of many Waters, although there be none. He warmeth Waters, and discovereth Baths. He was of the Order of Potestates, or Powers, before his fall, as he declared unto the King Solomon. He governeth 48 Legions of Spirits. His Seal is this, the which wear thou as aforesaid.

(50.) FURCAS.—The Fiftieth Spirit is Furcas. He is a Knight, and appeareth in the Form of a Cruel Old Man with a long Beard and a hoary Head, riding upon a pale-coloured Horse, with a Sharp Weapon in his hand. His Office is to teach the Arts of Philosophy, Astrology, Rhetoric, Logic, Cheiromancy, and Pyromancy, in all their parts, and perfectly. He hath under his Power 20 Legions of Spirits. His Seal, or Mark, is thus made, etc.

(51.) BALAM.—The Fifty-first Spirit is Balam or Balaam. He is a Terrible, Great, and Powerful King. He appeareth with three Heads: the first is like that of a Bull; the second is like that of a Man; the third is like that of a Ram. He hath the Tail of a Serpent, and Flaming Eyes. He rideth upon a furious Bear, and carrieth a Boshawk upon his Fist. He speaketh with a hoarse Voice, giving True Answers of Things Past, Present, and to Come. He maketh men to go Invisible, and also to be Witty. He governeth 40 Legions of Spirits. His Seal is this, etc.

(52.) ALLOCES.—The Fifty-second Spirit is Alloces, or Alocas. He is a Duke, Great, Mighty, and Strong, appearing in the Form of a Soldier[1] riding upon a Great Horse. His Face is like that of a Lion, very Red, and having Flaming Eyes. His Speech is hoarse and very big.[2] His Office is to teach the Art of Astronomy, and all the Liberal Sciences. He bringeth unto thee Good Familiars; also he ruleth over 36 Legions of Spirits. His Seal is this, which, etc.

(53.) CAMIO or CAIM.—The Fifty-third Spirit is Camio, or Caim. He is a Great President, and appeareth in the Form of the Bird called a Thrush at first, but afterwards he putteth on the Shape of a Man carrying in his Hand a Sharp Sword. He seemeth to answer in Burning Ashes, or in Coals of Fire. He is a Good Disputer. His Office is to give unto Men the Understanding of all Birds, Lowing of Bullocks, Barking of Dogs, and other Creatures; and also of the Voice of the Waters. He giveth True Answers of Things to Come. He was of the Order of Angels, but now ruleth over 30 Legions of Spirits Infernal. His Seal is this, which wear thou, etc.

(54.) MURMUR, or MURMUS.—The Fifty-fourth Spirit is called Murmur, or Murmus, or Murmux. He is a Great Duke, and an Earl; and appeareth in the Form of a Warrior riding upon a Gryphon, with a Ducal Crown upon his Head. There do go before him those his Min-

---

[1] Or Warrior.
[2] Thus expressed in the Codices.

isters with great Trumpets sounding. His Office is to teach Philosophy perfectly, and to constrain Souls Deceased to come before the Exorcist to answer those questions which he may wish to put to them, if desired. He was partly of the Order of Thrones, and partly of that of Angels. He now ruleth 30 Legions of Spirits. And his Seal is this, etc.

(55.) OROBAS.—The Fifty-fifth Spirit is Orobas. He is a great and Mighty Prince, appearing at first like a Horse; but after the command of the Exorcist he putteth on the Image of a Man. His Office is to discover all things Past, Present, and to Come; also to give Dignities, and Prelacies, and the Favour of Friends and of Foes. He giveth True Answers of Divinity, and of the Creation of the World. He is very faithful unto the Exorcist, and will not suffer him to be tempted of any Spirit. He governeth 20 Legions of Spirits. His Seal is this, etc.

(56.) GREMORY, or GAMORI.—The Fifty-sixth Spirit is Gremory, or Gamori. He is a Duke Strong and Powerful, and appeareth in the Form of a Beautiful Woman, with a Duchess's Crown tied about her waist, and riding on a Great Camel. His Office is to tell of all Things Past, Present, and to Come; and of Treasures Hid, and what they lie in; and to procure the Love of Women both Young and Old. He governeth 26 Legions of Spirits, and his Seal is this, etc.

(57.) OSÉ, or VOSO.—The Fifty-seventh Spirit is Oso, Osé, or Voso. He is a Great President, and appeareth like a Leopard at the first, but after a little time he putteth on the Shape of a Man. His Office is to make one cunning in the Liberal Sciences, and to give True Answers of Divine and Secret Things; also to change a Man into any Shape that the Exorcist pleaseth, so that

THE LESSER KEY 41

he that is so changed will not think any other thing than that he is in verity that Creature or Thing he is changed into. He governeth 30[1] Legions of Spirits, and this is his Seal, etc.

(58.) AMY, or AVNAS.—The Fifty-eighth Spirit is Amy, or Avnas. He is a Great President, and appeareth at first in the Form of a Flaming Fire; but after a while he putteth on the Shape of a Man. His office is to make one Wonderful Knowing[2] in Astrology and all the Liberal Sciences. He giveth Good Familiars, and can bewray Treasure that is kept by Spirits. He governeth 36 Legions of Spirits, and his Seal is this, etc.

(59.) ORIAX, or ORIAS.—The Fifty-ninth Spirit is Oriax, or Orias. He is a Great Marquis, and appeareth in the Form of a Lion,[3] riding upon a Horse Mighty and Strong, with a Serpent's Tail;[4] and he holdeth in his Right Hand two Great Serpents hissing. His Office is to teach the Virtues of the Stars, and to know the Mansions of the Planets, and how to understand their Virtues. He also transformeth Men, and he giveth Dignities, Prelacies, and Confirmation thereof; also Favour with Friends and with Foes. He doth govern 30 Legions of Spirits; and his Seal is this, etc.

(60.) VAPULA, or NAPHULA.—The Sixtieth Spirit is Vapula, or Naphula. He is a Duke Great, Mighty, and Strong; appearing in the Form of a Lion with Gryphon's Wings. His Office is to make Men Knowing in all Handcrafts and Professions, also in Philosophy, and other Sciences. He governeth 36 Legions of Spirits, and

---

[1] Should be 30. For these 72 Great Spirits of the Book Goetia are all Princes and Leaders of numbers.
[2] Thus in the actual Text.
[3] Or "with the Face of a Lion."
[4] The horse, or the Markis?—ED.

his Seal or Character is thus made, and thou shalt wear it as aforesaid, etc.

(61.) ZAGAN.—The Sixty-first Spirit is Zagan. He is a Great King and President, appearing at first in the Form of a Bull with Gryphon's Wings; but after a while he putteth on Human Shape. He maketh Men Witty. He can turn Wine into Water, and Blood into Wine, also Water into Wine. He can turn all Metals into Coin of the Dominion that Metal is of. He can even make Fools wise. He governeth 33 Legions of Spirits, and his Seal is this, etc.

(62.) VOLAC, or VALAK, or VALU, or UALAC.—The Sixty-second Spirit is Volac, or Valak, or Valu. He is a President Mighty and Great, and appeareth like a Child with Angel's Wings, riding on a Two-headed Dragon. His Office is to give True Answers of Hidden Treasures, and to tell where Serpents may be seen. The which he will bring unto the Exorciser without any Force or Strength being by him employed. He governeth 38 Legions of Spirits, and his Seal is thus.

(63.) ANDRAS.—The Sixty-third Spirit is Andras. He is a Great Marquis, appearing in the Form of an Angel with a Head like a Black Night Raven, riding upon a strong Black Wolf, and having a Sharp and Bright Sword flourished aloft in his hand. His Office is to sow Discords. If the Exorcist have not a care, he will slay both him and his fellows. He governeth 30 Legions of Spirits, and this is his Seal, etc.

(64.) HAURES, or HAURAS, or HAVRES, or FLAUROS.—The Sixty-fourth Spirit is Haures, or Hauras, or Havres, or Flauros. He is a Great Duke, and appeareth at first like a Leopard, Mighty, Terrible, and Strong, but after a while, at the Command of the Exorcist, he putteth on Human Shape with Eyes Flaming and Fiery, and a most Terrible Countenance. He giveth True Answers of all things, Present, Past, and to Come. But if he be not commanded into a Triangle, $\triangle$, he will Lie in all these Things, and deceive and beguile the Exorcist in these things, or in such and such business. He will, lastly, talk of the Creation of the World, and of Divinity, and of how he and other Spirits fell. He destroyeth and burneth up those who be the Enemies of the Exorcist should he so desire it; also he will not suffer him to be tempted by any other Spirit or otherwise. He governeth 36 Legions of Spirits, and his Seal is this, to be worn as a Lamen, etc.

(65.) ANDREALPHUS.—The Sixty-fifth Spirit is Andrealphus. He is a Mighty Marquis, appearing at first in the form of a Peacock, with great Noises. But after a time he putteth on Human shape. He can teach Geometry perfectly. He maketh Men very subtle therein; and in all Things pertaining unto Mensuration or Astronomy. He can transform a Man into the Likeness of a Bird. He governeth 30 Legions of Infernal Spirits, and his Seal is this, etc.

(66.) CIMEJES, or CIMEIES, or KIMARIS.—The Sixty-sixth Spirit is Cimejes, or Cimeies, or Kimaris. He is a Marquis, Mighty, Great, Strong and Powerful, appearing like a Valiant Warrior riding upon a goodly Black Horse. He ruleth over all Spirits in the parts of Africa. His Office is to teach perfectly Grammar, Logic, Rhetoric, and to discover things Lost or Hidden, and Treasures. He governeth 20 Legions of Infernals; and his Seal is this, etc.

(67.) AMDUSIAS, or AMDUKIAS.—The Sixty-seventh Spirit is Amdusias, or Amdukias. He is a Duke Great and Strong, appearing at first like a Unicorn, but at the request of the Exorcist he standeth before him in Human

Shape, causing Trumpets, and all manner of Musical Instruments to be heard, but not soon or immediately. Also he can cause Trees to bend and incline according to the Exorcist's Will. He giveth Excellent Familiars. He governeth 29 Legions of Spirits. And his Seal is this, etc.

(68.) BELIAL.—The Sixty-eighth Spirit is Belial. He is a Mighty and a Powerful King, and was created next after LUCIFER. He appeareth in the Form of Two Beautiful Angels sitting in a Chariot of Fire. He speaketh with a Comely Voice, and declareth that he fell first from among the worthier sort, that were before Michael, and other Heavenly Angels. His Office is to distribute Presentations and Senatorships, etc.; and to cause favour of Friends and of Foes. He giveth excellent Familiars, and governeth 50 Legions of Spirits. Note well that this King Belial must have Offerings, Sacrifices and Gifts presented unto him by the Exorcist, or else he will not give True Answers unto his Demands. But then he tarrieth not one hour in the Truth, unless he be constrained by Divine Power. And his Seal is this, which is to be worn as aforesaid, etc.

(69.) DECARABIA.—The Sixty-ninth Spirit is Decarabia. He appeareth in the Form of a Star in a Pentacle, at first; but after, at the command of the Exorcist, he putteth on the image of a Man. His Office is to discover the Virtues of Birds and Precious Stones, and to make the Similitude of all kinds of Birds to fly before the Exorcist, singing and drinking as natural Birds do. He governeth 30 Legions of Spirits, being himself a Great Marquis. And this is his Seal, which is to be worn, etc.

(70.) SEERE, SEAR, or SEIR.—The Seventieth Spirit is Seere, Sear, or Seir. He is a Mighty Prince, and Powerful, under AMAYMON, King of the East. He appeareth

THE LESSER KEY

in the Form of a Beautiful Man, riding upon a Winged Horse. His Office is to go and come; and to bring abundance of things to pass on a sudden, and to carry or re-carry anything whither thou wouldest have it to go, or whence thou wouldest have it from. He can pass over the whole Earth in the twinkling of an Eye. He giveth a True relation of all sorts of Theft, and of Treasure hid, and of many other things. He is of an indifferent Good Nature, and is willing to do anything which the Exorcist desireth. He governeth 26 Legions of Spirits. And this his Seal is to be worn, etc.

(71.) DANTALION.—The Seventy-first Spirit is Dantalion. He is a Duke Great and Mighty, appearing in the Form of a Man with many Countenances, all Men's and Women's Faces; and he hath a Book in his right hand. His Office is to teach all Arts and Sciences unto any; and to declare the Secret Counsel of any one; for he knoweth the Thoughts of all Men and Women, and can change them at his Will. He can cause Love, and show the Similitude of any person, and show the same by a Vision, let them be in what part of the World they Will. He governeth 36 Legions of Spirits; and this is his Seal, which wear thou, etc.

(72.) ANDROMALIUS.—The Seventy-second Spirit in Order is named Andromalius. He is an Earl, Great and Mighty, appearing in the Form of a Man holding a Great Serpent in his Hand. His Office is to bring back both a Thief, and the Goods which be stolen; and to discover all Wickedness, and Underhand Dealing; and to punish all Thieves and other Wicked People and also to discover Treasures that be Hid. He ruleth over 36 Legions of Spirits. His Seal is this, the which wear thou as aforesaid, etc.

THESE be the 72 Mighty Kings and Princes which King

Solomon Commanded into a Vessel of Brass, together with their Legions. Of whom BELIAL, BILETH, ASMODAY, and GAAP, were Chief. And it is to be noted that Solomon did this because of their pride, for he never declared other reason why he thus bound them. And when he had thus bound them up and sealed the Vessel, he by Divine Power did chase them all into a deep Lake or Hole in Babylon. And they of Babylon, wondering to see such a thing, they did then go wholly into the Lake, to break the Vessel open, expecting to find great store of Treasure therein. But when they had broken it open, out flew the Chief Spirits immediately, with their Legions following them; and they were all restored to their former places except BELIAL, who entered into a certain Image, and thence gave answers unto those who did offer Sacrifices unto him, and did worship the Image as their God, etc.

OBSERVATIONS.

FIRST, thou shalt know and observe the Moon's Age for thy working. The best days be when the Moon Luna is 2, 4, 6, 8, 10, 12, or 14 days old, as Solomon saith; and no other days be profitable. The Seals of the 72 Kings are to be made in Metals. The Chief Kings' in Sol (Gold); Marquises' in Luna (Silver); Dukes' in Venus (Copper); Prelacies' in Jupiter (Tin); Knights' in Saturn (Lead); Presidents' in Mercury (Mercury); Earls' in Venus (Copper), and Luna (Silver), alike equal, etc. THESE 72 Kings be under the Power of AMAYMON, CORSON, ZIMIMAY or ZIMINAIR, and GÖAP, who are the Four Great Kings ruling in the Four Quarters, or Cardinal Points,[1] viz.: East, West, North, and South, and are not

[1] These four Great Kings are usually called Oriens, or Uriens, Paymon or Paymonia, Ariton or Egyn, and Amaymon or Amaimon. By the Rabbins they are frequently entitled: Samael, Azazel, Azäel, and Mahazael.

THE LESSER KEY

to be called forth except it be upon Great Occasions; but are to be Invocated and Commanded to send such or such a Spirit that is under their Power and Rule, as is shown in the following Invocations or Conjurations. And the Chief Kings may be bound from 9 till 12 o'clock at Noon, and from 3 till Sunset; Marquises may be bound from 3 in the afternoon till 9 at Night, and from 9 at Night till Sunrise; Dukes may be bound from Sunrise till Noonday in Clear Weather; Prelates may be bound any hour of the Day; Knights may from Dawning of Day till Sunrise, or from 4 o'clock till Sunset; Presidents may be bound any time, excepting Twilight, at Night, unless the King whom they are under be Invocated; and Counties or Earls any hour of the Day, so it be in Woods, or in any other places whither men resort not, or where no noise is, etc.

CLASSIFIED LIST OF THE 72 CHIEF SPIRITS OF THE GOETIA, ACCORDING TO RESPECTIVE RANK.

(Seal in Gold.) KINGS.—(1.) Bael; (9.) Paimon; (13.) Beleth; (20.) Purson; (32.) Asmoday; (45.) Viné; (51.) Balam; (61.) Zagan; (68.) Belial.

(Seal in Copper.) DUKES.—(2.) Agares; (6.) Valefor; (8.) Barbatos; (11.) Gusion; (15.) Eligos; (16.) Zepar; (18.) Bathim; (19.) Sallos; (23.) Aim; (26.) Buné; (28.) Berith; (29.) Astaroth; (41.) Focalor; (42.) Vepar; (47.) Vual; (49.) Crocell; (52.) Alloces; (54.) Murmur; (56.) Gremory; (60.) Vapula; (64.) Haures; (67.) Amdusias; (71.) Dantalion.

(Seal in Tin.) PRINCES AND PRELATES.—(3.) Vassago; (12.) Sitri; (22.) Ipos; (33.) Gäap; (36.) Stolas; (55.) Orobas; (70.) Seere.

(Seal in Silver.) MARQUISES.—(4.) Samigina; (7.) Amon; (14.) Lerajé; (24.) Naberius; (27.) Ronové; (30.) Forneus; (35.) Marchosias; (37.) Phenex; (43.) Sabnock; (44.) Shax; (59.) Orias; (63.) Andras; (65.) Andrealphus; (66.) Cimeies; (69.) Decarabia.

(Seal in Mercury.) PRESIDENTS.—(5.) Marbas; (10.) Buer; (17.) Botis; (21.) Marax; (25.) Glasya-Labolas; (31.) Foras; (33.) Gäap; (39.) Malphas; (48.) Häagenti; (53.) Caïm; (57.) Ose; (58.) Amy; (61.) Zagan; (62.) Valac.

(Seal in Copper and Silver alike equal.) EARLS, or COUNTS.—(17.) Botis; (21.) Marax; (25.) Glasya-Labolas; (27.) Ronové; (34.) Furfur; (38.) Halphas; (40.) Räum; (45.) Viné; (46.) Bifrons; (72.) Andromalius.

(Seal in Lead.) KNIGHTS.—(50.) Furcas.

NOTE.—It will be remarked that several among the above Spirits possess two titles of different ranks; *e.g.*, (45.) Viné is both King and Earl; (25.) Glasya-Labolas is both President and Earl, etc. "Prince" and "Prelate" are apparently used as interchangeable terms. Probably the Seals of Earls should be made of Iron, and those of Presidents in mixture either of Copper and Silver, or of Silver and Mercury; as otherwise the Metal of one Planet, Mars, is excluded from the List; the Metals attributed to the Seven Planets being: to Saturn, Lead; to Jupiter, Tin; to Mars, Iron; to the Sun, Gold; to Venus, Copper; to Mercury, Mercury and mixtures of Metals, and to Luna, Silver.

IN a manuscript codex by Dr. Rudd, which is in the British Museum, Hebrew names of these 72 Spirits are given; but it appears to me that many are manifestly incorrect in orthography. The codex in question, though beautifully written, also contains many other errors, particularly in the Sigils. Such as they are, these names in

THE LESSER KEY 49

the Hebrew of Dr. Rudd are here shown. (*See Figures 81 to 152 inclusive.*)

THE MAGICAL CIRCLE.

THIS is the Form of the Magical Circle of King Solomon, the which he made that he might preserve himself therein from the malice of these Evil Spirits. (*See Frontispiece, Figure* 153.) This Magical Circle is to be made 9 feet across, and the Divine Names are to be written around it, beginning at EHYEH, and ending at LEVANAH, Luna.

(Colours.—The space between the outer and inner circles, where the serpent is coiled, with the Hebrew names written along his body, is bright deep yellow. The square in the centre of the circle, where the word "Master" is written, is filled in with red. All names and letters are in black. In the Hexagrams the outer triangles where the letters A, D, O, N, A, I, appear are filled in with bright yellow, the centres, where the T-shaped crosses are, blue or green. In the Pentagrams outside the circle, the outer triangles where "Te, tra, gram, ma, ton," is written, are filled in bright yellow, and the centres with the T crosses written therein are red.[1])

THE MAGICAL TRIANGLE OF SOLOMON.

THIS is the Form of the Magical Triangle, into the which Solomon did command the Evil Spirits. It is to be made at 2 feet distance from the Magical Circle and it is 3 feet across. (*See Frontispiece Figure* 154.) Note

[1] The coiled serpent is only shown in one private codex, the Hebrew names being in most cases simply written round in a somewhat spiral arrangement within the double circle. It is to be remembered that Hebrew is always written from right to left,

that this triangle is to be placed toward that quarter whereunto the Spirit belongeth. And the base of the triangle is to be nearest unto the Circle, the apex pointing in the direction of the quarter of the Spirit. Observe thou also the Moon in thy working, as aforesaid, etc. Anaphaxeton is sometimes written Anepheneton.

(Colours.—Triangle outlined in black; name of Michael black on white ground; the three Names without the triangle written in red; circle in centre entirely filled in in dark green.)

THE HEXAGRAM OF SOLOMON.

This is the Form of the Hexagram of Solomon, the figure whereof is to be made on parchment of a calf's skin, and worn at the skirt of thy white vestment, and covered with a cloth of fine linen white and pure, the which is to be shown unto the Spirits when they do appear, so that they be compelled to take human shape upon them and be obedient.

(Colours.—Circle, Hexagon, and T cross in centre outlined in black, Maltese crosses black; the five exterior

instead of from left to right like ordinary European languages. The small Maltese crosses are placed to mark the conclusion of each separate set of Hebrew names. These names are those of Deity Angels and Archangels allotted by the Qabalists to each of the 9 first Sephiroth or Divine Emanations. In English letters they run thus, beginning from the head of the serpent: + Ehyeh Kether Metatron Chaioth Ha-Qadehs Rashith Ha-Galgalim S.P.M. (for "Sphere of the Primum Mobile") + Iah Chokmah Ratziel Auphanim Masloth S.S.F (for "Sphere of the Fixed Stars," or S.Z. for "Sphere of the Zodiac") + Iehovah Eolhim Binah Tzaphquiel Aralim Shabbathai S. (for "Sphere") of Saturn + El Chesed Tzadquiel Chaschmalim Tzedeq S. of Jupiter + Elohim Gibor Geburah Kamael Seraphim Madim S. of Mars + Iehovah Eloah Va-Daäth Tiphereth Raphaël Malakim Shemesh S. of the Sun + Iehovah Tzabaoth Netzach Haniel Elohim Nogah S. of Venus. + Elohim Tzabaoth Hod Michaël Beni Elohim Kokav S. of Mercury + Shaddaï El Chai Iesod Gabriel Cherubim Levanah S. of the Moon +.

THE LESSER KEY 51

triangles of the Hexagram where Te, tra, gram, ma, ton, is written, are filled in with bright yellow; the T cross in centre is red, with the three little squares therein in black. The lower exterior triangle, where the Sigil is drawn in black, is left white. The words "Tetragrammaton" and "Tau" are in black letters; and AGLA with Alpha and Omega in red letters.)

THE PENTAGRAM OF SOLOMON.

THIS is the Form of Pentagram of Solomon, the figure whereof is to be made in Sol or Luna (Gold or Silver), and worn upon thy breast; having the Seal of the Spirit required upon the other side thereof. It is to preserve thee from danger, and also to command the Spirits by.

(Colours.—Circle and pentagram outlined in black. Names and Sigils within Pentagram black also. "Tetragrammaton" in red letters. Ground of centre of Pentagram, where "Soluzen" is written, green. External angles of Pentagram where "Abdia," "Ballaton," "Halliza," etc., are written, blue.)

THE MAGIC RING OR DISC OF SOLOMON.

THIS is the Form of the Magic Ring, or rather Disc, of Solomon, the figure whereof is to be made in gold or silver. It is to be held before the face of the exorcist to preserve him from the stinking sulphurous fumes and flaming breath of the Evil Spirits.

(Colour.—Bright yellow. Letters, black.)

THE VESSEL OF BRASS.

THIS is the Form of the Vessel of Brass wherein King Solomon did shut up the Evil Spirits, etc. (*See Figures* 158 *and* 159.) (Somewhat different forms are given in the various codices. The seal in Figure 160 was made in brass to cover this vessel with at the top. This history of the genii shut up in the brazen vessel by King Solomon recalls the story of "The Fisherman and the Jinni" in "The Arabian Nights." In this tale, however, there was only one jinni shut up in a vessel of yellow brass the which was covered at the top with a leaden seal. This jinni tells the fisherman that his name is Sakhr, or Sacar.)

(Colour.—Bronze. Letters.—Black on a red band.)

THE SECRET SEAL OF SOLOMON.

THIS is the Form of the Secret Seal of Solomon, wherewith he did bind and seal up the aforesaid Spirits with their legions in the Vessel of Brass.

This seal is to be made by one that is clean both inwardly and outwardly, and that hath not defiled himself by any woman in the space of a month, but hath in prayer and fasting desired of God to forgive him all his sins, etc.

It is to be made on the day of Mars or Saturn (Tuesday or Saturday) at night at 12 o'clock, and written upon virgin parchment with the blood of a black cock that never trode hen. Note that on this night the moon must be increasing in light (*i.e.*, going from new to full) and in the Zodiacal Sign of Virgo. And when the seal is so made thou shalt perfume it with alum, raisins dried in the sun, dates, cedar and lignum aloes.

Also, by this seal King Solomon did command all the aforesaid Spirits in the Vessel of Brass, and did seal it up with this same seal. He by it gained the love of all manner of persons, and overcame in battle, for neither weapons, nor fire, nor water could hurt him. And this

THE LESSER KEY

privy seal was made to cover the vessel at the top withal, etc.

Note: Figures 162 to 174 inclusive are interesting as showing a marked resemblance to the central design of the Secret Seal. It will be observed that the evident desire is to represent hieroglyphically a person raising his or her hands in adoration. Nearly all are stone sepulchral steles, and the execution of them is rough and primitive in the extreme. Most are in the Musëe du Louvre at Paris.

Figures 162 and 163 are from the district of Constantine and show a figure raising its arms in adoration.

In Figure 164, also from Constantine, the person bears a palm branch in the right hand. Above is a hieroglyphic representing either the Lunar Disc or the Sun in the heavens; but more probably the former.

Figure 165 is a more complicated stele. Above is the symbol already mentioned, then comes the sign of the Pentagram, represented by a five-pointed star, towards which the person raises his or her hands. Besides the latter is a rude form of caduceus. A brief inscription follows in the Punic character. The Punic or Carthaginian language is usually considered to have been a dialect of Phœnician, and Carthage was of course a colony of Tyre. Beneath the Tunic inscription is a horse's head in better drawing than the sculpture of the rest of the stele, which would seem to imply that the rudeness of the representation of the human figure is intentional. This and the following stele are also from Constantine.

In Figure 166 again, the horse is best delineated by far. In addition to the other symbols there is either a hand or a foot, for it is almost impossible to distinguish which, at the head of the stele, followed by an egg-and-tongue moulding. The figure of the person with the arms raised is treated as a pure hieroglyphic and is placed between two rude caducei. The Lunar or Solar Symbol follows.

Figure 167, also from Constantine, shows the last-mentioned symbol above. The figure with the arms raised is simply a hieroglyph, and is placed between an arm and hand on the one side, and a rude caduceus on the other.

Figure 168 shows the person holding a rude caduceus in the right hand, and standing above a dolphin. This latter, as in the case of the horse in 165 and 166, is by far the best delineated.

Figure 169, this also being from Constantine, shows the usual human hieroglyph between a caduceus and a crescent.

Figure 170 is from the site of ancient Carthage. It is very rough in workmanship, and the designs are mere scratchings on the stone. The *ensemble* has the effect of an evil Sigil.

Figure 171 is also from Carthage and the various symbols appear to have become compressed into and synthesised in the form of a peculiarly evil-looking caduceus.

Figure 172 is from the decoration of a sepulchral urn found at Oldenburgh in Germany. It is remarkable as showing the same hieroglyphic human form with the crescent above; the latter in the Secret Seal of Solomon has a flattened top, and is therefore more like a bowl, and is placed across the hieroglyph.

Figure 173 is an Egyptian design which would show an analogy between the symbol and the idea of the force of the creation.

Figure 174 is a stele from Phœnicia somewhat similar to the others, except that the rudimentary caducei in Figures 166 and 170 are here replaced by two roughly drawn Ionic columns.

These last three designs are taken from the work of the Chevalier Emile Soldi-Colbert de Beaulieu, on the "*Langue Sacrée.*"

In Figure 175 is given the Seal of the Spirit HALAHEL. This Spirit is said to be under the rule of BAEL, and to be of a mixed nature, partly good and partly evil, like the spirits of Theurgia-Goetia which follow in the second book of the Lemegeton.

THE OTHER MAGICAL REQUISITES.

THE other magical requisites are: a sceptre, a sword, a mitre, a cap, a long white robe of linen, and other garments for the purpose;[1] also a girdle of lion's skin three inches broad, with all the names written about it which be round the outmost part of the Magical Circle. Also perfumes, and a chafing-dish of charcoal kindled to put the fumes on, to smoke or perfume the place appointed for action; also anointing oil to anoint thy temples and thine eyes with; and fair water to wash thyself in. And in so doing, thou shalt say as David said:

THE ADORATION AT THE BATH.

"Thou shalt purge me with hyssop, O Lord! and I shall be clean: Thou shalt wash me, and I shall be whiter than snow."

And at the putting on of thy garments thou shalt say: THE ADORATION AT THE INDUING OF THE VESTMENTS.

"By the figurative mystery of these holy vestures (or of this holy vestment) I will clothe me with the armour of salvation in the strength of the Most High, ANCHOR;

---

[1] In many Codices it is written "a sceptre or sword, a mitre or cap." By the "other garments" would be meant not only undergarments, but also mantles of different colours.

AMACOR; AMIDES; THEODINIAS; ANITOR; that my desired end may be effected through Thy strength, O ADONAI! unto Whom the praise and glory will for ever and ever belong! Amen!"

After thou hast so done, make prayers unto God according unto thy work, as Solomon hath commanded.

THE CONJURATION TO CALL FORTH ANY OF THE AFORESAID SPIRITS.

I DO invoke and conjure thee, O Spirit, N.[1]; and being with power armed from the SUPREME MAJESTY, I do strongly command thee, by BERALANENSIS, BALDACHIENSIS, PAUMACHIA, and APOLOGIAE SEDES; by the most Powerful Princes, Genii, Liachidæ, and Ministers of the Tartarean Abode; and by the Chief Prince of the Seat of Apologia in the Ninth Legion, I do invoke thee, and by invocating conjure thee. And being armed with power from the SUPREME MAJESTY, I do strongly command thee, by Him Who spake and it was done, and unto whom all creatures be obedient. Also I, being made after the image of GOD, endued with power from GOD and created according unto His will, do exorcise thee by that most mighty and powerful name of GOD, EL, strong and wonderful; O thou Spirit N. And I command thee and Him who spake the Word and HIS FIAT was accomplished, and by all the names of God. Also by the names ADONAI, EL, ELOHIM, ELOHI, EHYEH, ASHER EHYEH, ZABAOTH, ELION, IAH, TETRAGRAMMATON, SHADDAI, LORD GOD MOST HIGH, I do exorcise thee and do powerfully command thee, O thou Spirit N., that thou dost forth-

[1] Here interpolate the name of the Spirit desired to be invocated. In some of the Codices there are faint variations in the form of wording of the conjurations, but not sufficient to change the sense, *e. g.*, "Tartarean abode" for "Tartarean seat," etc.

with appear unto me here before this Circle in a fair human shape, without any deformity or tortuosity. And by this ineffable name, TETRAGRAMMATON IEHOVAH, do I command thee, at the which being heard the elements are overthrown, the air is shaken, the sea runneth back, the fire is quenched, the earth trembleth, and all the hosts of the celestials, terrestrials, and infernals do tremble together, and are troubled and confounded. Wherefore come thou, O Spirit N., forthwith, and without delay, from any or all parts of the world wherever thou mayest be, and make rational answers unto all things that I shall demand of thee. Come thou peaceably, visibly, and affably, now, and without delay, manifesting that which I shall desire. For thou art conjured by the name of the LIVING and TRUE GOD, HELIOREN, wherefore fulfil thou my commands, and persist thou therein unto the end, and according unto mine interest, visibly and affably speaking unto me with a voice clear and intelligible without any ambiguity.

REPEAT this conjuration as often as thou pleasest, and if the Spirit come not yet, say as followeth:

THE SECOND CONJURATION.

I DO invocate, conjure, and command thee, O thou Spirit N., to appear and to show thyself visibly unto me before this Circle in fair and comely shape, without any deformity or tortuosity; by the name and in the name IAH and VAU, which Adam heard and spake; and by the name of GOD, AGLA, which Lot heard and was saved with his family; and by the name IOTH, which Jacob heard from the angel wrestling with him, and was delivered from the hand of Esau his brother; and by the name ANAPHAXETON which Aaron heard and spake and was made wise; and by the name ZABAOTH, which Moses named and all the rivers were turned into blood; and by the name ASHER EHYEH ORISTON, which Moses named, and all the rivers brought forth frogs, and they ascended into the houses, destroying all things; and by the name ELION, which Moses named, and there was great hail such as had not been since the beginning of the world; and by the name ADONAI, which Moses named, and there came up locusts, which appeared upon the whole land, and devoured all which the hail had left; and by the name SCHEMA AMATHIA which Ioshua called upon, and the sun stayed his course; and by the name ALPHA and OMEGA, which Daniel named, and destroyed Bel, and slew the Dragon; and in the name EMMANUEL, which the three children, Shadrach, Meshach and Abed-nego, sang in the midst of the fiery furnace, and were delivered; and by the name HAGIOS; and by the SEAL[1] OF ADONI; and by ISCHYROS, ATHANATOS, PARACLETOS; and by O THEOS, ICTROS, ATHANATOS; and by these three secret names, AGLA, ON, TETRAGRAMMATON, do I adjure and constrain thee. And by these names, and by all the other names of the LIVING and TRUE GOD, the LORD ALMIGHTY, I do exorcise and command thee, O Spirit N., even by Him Who spake the Word and it was done, and to Whom all creatures are obedient; and by the dreadful judgments of GOD; and by the uncertain Sea of Glass, which is before the DIVINE MAJESTY, mighty and powerful; by the four beasts before the throne, having eyes before and behind; by the fire round about the throne; by the holy angels of Heaven; and by the mighty wisdom of GOD; I do potently exorcise thee, that thou appearest here before this Circle, to fulfil my will in all things which shall

---

[1] In some "By the Seat of Adonai" or "By the Throne of Adonai." In these conjurations and elsewhere in the body of the text I have given the divine names correctly.

seem good unto me; by the Seal of BASDATHEA BALDA-CHIA; and by this name PRIMEUMATON, which Moses named, and the earth opened, and did swallow up Kora, Dathan, and Abiram. Wherefore thou shalt make faithful answers unto all my demands, O Spirit N., and shalt perform all my desires so far as in thine office thou art capable hereof. Wherefore, come thou, visibly, peaceably, and affably, now without delay, to manifest that which I desire, speaking with a clear and perfect voice, intelligibly, and to mine understanding.

IF HE come not yet at the rehearsal of these two first conjurations (but without doubt he will), say on as followeth; it being a constraint:

THE CONSTRAINT.

I DO conjure thee, O thou Spirit N., by all the most glorious and efficacious names of the MOST GREAT AND INCOMPREHENSIBLE LORD GOD OF HOSTS, that thou comest quickly and without delay from all parts and places of the earth and world wherever thou mayest be, to make rational answers unto my demands, and that visibly and affably, speaking with a voice intelligible unto mine understanding as aforesaid. I conjure and constrain thee, O thou Spirit N., by all the names aforesaid; and in addition by these seven great names wherewith Solomon the Wise bound thee and thy companions in a Vessel of Brass, ADONAI, PREYAI or PRERAI, TETRAGRAMMATON, ANAPHAXETON or ANEPHENETON, INESSENFATOAL or INESSENFATALL, PATHTUMON or PATHATUMON, and ITEMON; that thou appearest here before this Circle to fulfil my will in all things that seem good unto me. And if thou be still so disobedient, and refusest still to come, I will in the power and by the power of the name of the SUPREME AND EVERLASTING LORD GOD WHO created both thee and me and all the world in six days, and what is contained therein, EIE, SARAYE, and by the power of this name PRIMEUMATON which commandeth the whole host of Heaven, curse thee, and deprive thee of thine office, joy, and place, and bind thee in the depths of the Bottomless Pit or Abyss, there to remain unto the Day of the Last Judgment. And I will bind thee in the Eternal Fire, and into the Lake of Flame and of Brimstone, unless thou comest quickly and appearest here before this Circle to do my will. Therefore, come thou! in and by the holy names ADONAI, ZABAOTH, ADONAI, AMIORAN. Come thou! for it is ADONAI who commandest thee.

IF THOU hast come thus far, and yet he appeareth not, thou mayest be sure that he is sent unto some other place by his King, and cannot come; and if it be so, invocate the King as here followeth, to send him. But if he do not come still, then thou mayest be sure that he is bound in chains in hell, and that he is not in the custody of his King. If so, and thou still hast a desire to call him even from thence, thou must rehearse the general curse which is called the Spirits' Chain.

Here followeth, therefore, the Invocation of the King:[1]

THE INVOCATION OF THE KING.

O THOU great, powerful, and mighty KING AMAIMON, who bearest rule by the power of the SUPREME GOD EL over all spirits both superior and inferior of the Infernal Orders in the Dominion of the East; I do invocate and command thee by the especial and true name of GOD; and by that God that Thou Worshippest; and by the Seal of thy creation; and by the most mighty and powerful name of GOD, IEHOVAH TETRAGRAMMATON who cast

---

[1] It will depend on the quarter to which the Spirit is attributed, which of the four chief kings are to be invoked.

THE LESSER KEY 61

thee out of heaven with all other infernal spirits; and by all the most powerful and great names of GOD who created Heaven, and Earth, and Hell, and all things in them contained; and by their power and virtue; and by the name PRIMEUMATON who commandeth the whole host of Heaven; that thou mayest cause, enforce, and compel the Spirit N. to come unto me here before this Circle in a fair and comely shape, without harm unto me or unto any other creature, to answer truly and faithfully unto all my requests; so that I may accomplish my will and desire in knowing or obtaining any matter or thing which by office thou knowest is proper for him to perform or accomplish, through the power of GOD, EL, Who created and doth dispose of all things both celestial, aërial, terrestrial, and infernal.

AFTER thou shalt have invocated the King in this manner twice or thrice over, then conjure the spirit thou wouldst call forth by the aforesaid conjurations, rehearsing them several times together, and he will come without doubt, if not at the first or second time of rehearsing. But if he do not come, add the "Spirits' Chain" unto the end of the aforesaid conjurations, and he will be forced to come, even if he be bound in chains, for the chains must break off from him, and he will be at liberty:

THE GENERAL CURSE, CALLED THE SPIRITS' CHAIN, AGAINST ALL SPIRITS THAT REBEL.

O THOU wicked and disobedient spirit N., because thou hast rebelled, and hast not obeyed nor regarded my words which I have rehearsed; they being all glorious and incomprehensible names of the true GOD, the maker and creator of thee and of me, and of all the world; I DO by the power of these names the which no creature is able to resist, curse thee into the depth of the Bottomless Abyss, there to remain unto the Day of Doom in chains, and in fire and brimstone unquenchable, unless thou forthwith appear here before this Circle, in this triangle to do my will. And, therefore, come thou quickly and peaceably, in and by these names of GOD, ADONAI, ZABAOTH, ADONAI, AMIORAN; come thou! come thou! for it is the King of Kings, even ADONAI, who commandeth thee.

WHEN thou shalt have rehearsed thus far, but still he cometh not, then write thou his seal on parchment and put thou it into a strong black box;[1] with brimstone, assafœtida, and such like things that bear a stinking smell; and then bind the box up round with an iron wire, and hang it upon the point of thy sword, and hold it over the fire of charcoal; and say as followeth unto the fire first, it being placed toward that quarter whence the Spirit is to come:

THE CONJURATION OF THE FIRE.

I CONJURE thee, O fire, by him who made thee and all other creatures for good in the world, that thou torment, burn, and consume this Spirit N., for everlasting. I condemn thee, thou Spirit N., because thou art disobedient and obeyest not my commandment, nor keepest the precepts of the LORD THY GOD, neither wilt thou obey me nor mine invocations, having thereby called thee forth, I, who am the servant of the MOST HIGH AND IMPERIAL LORD GOD OF HOSTS, IEHOVAH, I who am digni-

---

[1] This box should evidently be in metal or in something which does not take fire easily.

fied and fortified by His celestial power and permission, and yet thou comest not to answer these my propositions here made unto thee. For the which thine averseness and contempt thou art guilty of great disobedience and rebellion, and therefore shall I excommunicate thee, and destroy thy name and seal, the which I have enclosed in this box; and shall burn thee in the immortal fire and bury thee in immortal oblivion; unless thou immediately come and appear visibly and affably, friendly and courteously here unto me before this Circle, in this triangle, in a form comely and fair, and in no wise terrible, hurtful, or frightful to me or any other creature whatsoever upon the face of earth. And thou shalt make rational answers unto my requests, and perform all my desires in all things, that I shall make unto thee.

AND if he come not even yet, thou shalt say as followeth:

THE GREATER CURSE.[1]

Now, O thou Spirit N., since thou art still pernicious and disobedient, and wilt not appear unto me to answer unto such things as I would have desired of thee, or would have been satisfied in; I do in the name, and by the power and dignity of the Omnipresent and Immortal Lord God of Hosts IEHOVAH TETRAGRAMMATON, the only creator of Heaven, and Earth, and Hell, and all that is therein, who is the marvellous Disposer of all things both visible and invisible, curse thee, and deprive thee of all thine office, joy, and place; and I do bind thee in the depths of the Bottomless Abyss there to remain until the Day of Judgment, I say into the Lake of Fire and Brim-

---

[1] In some codices this is called ''the Curse'' only; but in one or two the ''Spirits' Chain'' is called ''the Lesser Curse,'' and this the ''Greater Curse.''

stone which is prepared for all rebellious, disobedient, obstinate, and pernicious spirits. Let all the company of Heaven curse thee! Let the sun, moon, and all the stars curse thee! Let the LIGHT and all the hosts of Heaven curse thee into the fire unquenchable, and into the torments unspeakable. And as thy name and seal contained in this box chained and bound up, shall be choken in sulphurous stinking substances, and burned in this material fire; so in the name IEHOVAH and by the power and dignity of these three names, TETRAGRAMMATON, ANAPHAXETON, and PRIMEUMATON, I do cast thee, O thou wicked and disobedient Spirit N., into the Lake of Fire which is prepared for the damnéd and accurséd spirits, and there to remain unto the day of doom, and never more to be remembered before the face of GOD, who shall come to judge the quick, and the dead, and the world, by fire.

THEN the exorcist must put the box into the fire, and by-and-by the Spirit will come, but as soon as he is come, quench the fire that the box is in, and make a sweet perfume, and give him welcome and a kind entertainment, showing unto him the Pentacle that is at the bottom of your vesture covered with a linen cloth, saying:

THE ADDRESS UNTO THE SPIRIT UPON HIS COMING.

BEHOLD thy confusion if thou refusest to be obedient! Behold the Pentacle of Solomon which I have brought here before thy presence! Behold the person of the exorcist in the midst of the exorcism; him who is arméd by GOD and without fear; him who potently invocateth thee and calleth thee forth unto appearance; even him, thy master, who is called OCTINIMOS. Wherefore make rational answer unto my demands, and prepare to be obedient unto thy master in the name of the Lord:

BATHAL OR VATHAT RUSHING UPON ABRAC!

ABEOR COMING UPON ABERER![1]

THEN he or they will be obedient, and bid thee ask what thou wilt, for he or they be subjected by God to fulfil our desires and commands. And when he or they shall have appeared and showed himself or themselves humble and meek, then shalt thou rehearse:

THE WELCOME UNTO THE SPIRIT.

WELCOME Spirit N., O most noble king [2] (or kings)! I say thou art welcome unto me, because I have called thee through Him who has created Heaven, and Earth, and Hell, and all that is in them contained, and because also thou hast obeyed. By that same power by the which I have called thee forth, I bind thee, that thou remain affably and visibly here before this Circle (or before this Circle and in this triangle) so constant and so long as I shall have occasion for thy presence; and not to depart without my license until thou hast duly and faithfully performed my will without any falsity.

THEN standing in the midst of the Circle, thou shall stretch forth thine hand in a gesture of command and say:

"BY THE PENTACLE OF SOLOMON HAVE I CALLED THEE! GIVE UNTO ME A TRUE ANSWER."

Then let the exorcist state his desires and requests.

And when the evocation is finished thou shalt license the Spirit to depart thus:

---

[1] In the Latin, "Bathal vel Vathat super Abrac ruens! Abeor veniens super Aberer!"

[2] Or whatever his dignity may be.

THE LICENSE TO DEPART.

O THOU Spirit N., because thou hast diligently answered unto my demands, and hast been very ready and willing to come at my call, I do here license thee to depart unto thy proper place; without causing harm or danger unto man or beast. Depart, then, I say, and be thou very ready to come at my call, being duly exorcised and conjured by the sacred rites of magic. I charge thee to withdraw peaceably and quietly, and the peace of GOD be ever continued between thee and me! AMEN!

AFTER thou hast given the Spirit license to depart, thou art not to go out of the circle until he or they be gone, and until thou shalt have made prayers and rendered thanks unto God for the great blessings He hath bestowed upon thee in granting thy desires, and delivering thee from all the malice of the enemy the devil.

Also note! Thou mayest command these spirits into the Vessel of Brass in the same manner as thou dost into the triangle, by saying: "that thou dost forthwith appear before this Circle, in this Vessel of Brass, in a fair and comely shape," etc., as hath been shown in the foregoing conjurations.

EXPLANATION OF CERTAIN NAMES USED IN THIS BOOK LEMEGETON.

Eheie. Kether.—Almighty God, whose dwelling is in the highest Heavens:

Haioth.—The great King of Heaven, and of all the powers therein:

Methratton.—And of all the holy hosts of Angels and Archangels:

Reschith.—Hear the prayers of Thy servant who putteth his trust in Thee:

Hagalgalim.—Let thy Holy Angels be commanded to assist me at this time and at all times.

Iehovah.—God Almighty, God Omnipotent, hear my prayer:

Hadonat.—Command Thy Holy Angels above the fixed stars:

Ophanim.—To be assisting and aiding Thy servant:

Iophiel.—That I may command all spirits of air, water, fire, earth, and hell:

Masloth.—So that it may tend unto Thy glory and unto the good of man.

Iehovah.—God Almighty, God Omnipotent, hear my prayer:

Elohim.—God with us, God be always present with us:

Binah.—Strengthen us and support us, both now and for ever:

Aralim.—In these our undertakings, which we perform but as instruments in Thy hands:

Zabbathi (should be Shabbathii).—In the hands of Thee, the great God of Sabäoth.

Hesel (should be Chesed).—Thou great God, governor and creator of the planets, and of the Host of Heaven:

Hasmalim (should be Chashmalim).—Command them by Thine almighty power:

Zelez (should be Zedeq).—To be now present and assisting to us Thy poor servants, both now and for ever.

Elohim Geber (should be Gibor).—Most Almighty and eternal and ever living Lord God:

Seraphim.—Command Thy seraphim:

Camael, Madim.—To attend on us now at this time, to assist us, and to defend us from all perils and dangers.

Eloha.—O Almighty God! be present with us both now and for ever:

Tetragrammaton.—And let thine Almighty power and presence ever guard and protect us now and for ever:

Raphael.—Let thy holy angel Raphael wait upon us at this present and for ever:

Schemes (or Shemesh).—To assist us in these our undertakings.

Iehovah.—God Almighty, God Omnipotent, hear my prayer:

Sabäoth.—Thou great God of Sabäoth:

Netzah (or Netzach).—All-seeing God:

Elohim.—God be present with us, and let thy presence be now and always present with us:

Haniel.—Let thy holy angel Haniel come and minister unto us at this present.

Sabäoth.—O thou great God of Sabäoth, be present with us at this time and for ever:

THE LESSER KEY

Hodben (should be Hod simply).—Let Thine Almighty power defend us and protect us, both now and for ever:

Michael.—Let Michael, who is, under Thee, general of thy heavenly host:

Cochab.—Come and expel all evil and danger from us both now and for ever.

Sadai.—Thou great God of all wisdom and knowledge:

Jesal (should be Iesod).—Instruct Thy poor and most humble servant:

Cherubim.—By Thy holy cherubim:

Gabriel.—By Thy Holy Angel Gabriel, who is the Author and Messenger of good tidings:

Levanah.—Direct and support us at this present and for ever.

The Explanation of the Two Triangles [1] in the Parchment.

Alpha And Omega.—Thou, O great God, Who art the beginning and the end:

Tetragrammaton.—Thou God of Almighty power, be ever present with us to guard and protect us, and let Thy Holy Spirit and presence be now and always with us:

Soluzen.—I command thee, thou Spirit of whatsoever region thou art, to come unto this circle:

Halliza.—And appear in human shape:

Bellator (or Ballaton).—And speak unto us audibly in our mother-tongue:

---

[1] Evidently meaning both the Hexagram and the Pentagram of Solomon. (*See Figures* 155 *and* 156.)

Bellonoy (or Bellony).—And show, and discover unto us all treasure that thou knowest of, or that is in thy keeping, and deliver it unto us quietly:

Hallii. Hra.—And answer all such questions as we may demand without any defect now at this time.

An Explanation of Solomon's Triangle

Anephezeton.—Thou great God of all the Heavenly Host:

Primeumaton.—Thou Who art the First and Last, let all spirits be subject unto us, and let the Spirit be bound in this triangle, which disturbs this place:

Michael.—By Thy Holy Angel Michael, until I shall discharge him.

(Here endeth this First Book of the Lemegeton, which is called the Goetia.)

Y^{se} Conjuratiouns of ye Booke Goetia in ye Lemegeton which Solomoun ye Kynge did give unto Lemuel hys sonne, rendered into ye Magicall or Angelike Language by our Illustrious and ever-Glorious Frater, ye Wise Perdurabo, that Myghtye Chiefe of ye Rosy-Cross Fraternitye, now sepulchred in ye Vault of ye Collegium S.S. And soe may we doe alle!

ATTE YE BATHES OF ART.

Asperges me, Domine, hyssopo, et mundabor: Lavabis me, et super nivem dealbabor.

ATTE YE INDUYNGE OF YE HOLY VESTURES.

In the mystery of these vestures of the Holy Ones, I gird up my power in the girdles of righteousness and truth in the power of the Most High: Ancor: Amacor: Amides: Theodonias: Anitor: let be mighty my power: let it endure for ever: in the power of Adonai, to whom the praise and the glory shall be; whose end cannot be.

YE FYRSTE CONJOURATIOUN.

I invoke and move thee, O thou, Spirit N.: and being exalted above ye in the power of the Most High, I say unto thee, Obey! in the name Beralensis, Baldachiensis, Paumachia, and Apologiae Sedes: and of the mighty ones who govern, spirits, Liachidae and ministers of the House of Death: and by the Chief Prince of the seat of Apologia in the Ninth Legion, I do invoke thee and by invoking conjure thee. And being exalted above ye in the power of the Most High, I say unto thee, Obey! in the name of him who spake and it was, to whom all creatures and things obey. Moreover I, whom God made in the likeness of God, who is the creator according to his living breath, stir thee up in the name which is the voice of wonder of the mighty God, El, strong and unspeakable, O thou Spirit N.

And I say to thee obey, in the name of him who spake and it was; and in every one of ye, O ye names of God! Moreover in the names Adonai, El, Elohim, Elohi, Ehyeh Asher Ehyeh, Zabaoth, Elion, Iah, Tetragrammaton, Shaddai, Lord God Most High, I stir thee up; and in our strength I say Obey! O Spirit N. Appear unto His servants in a moment; before the circle in the likeness of a man; and visit me in peace. And in the ineffable name Tetragrammaton Iehovah, I say, Obey! whose mighty sound being exalted in power the pillars are divided, the winds of the firmament groan aloud; the fire burns not; the earth moves in earthquakes; and all things of the house of heaven and earth and the dwelling-place of darkness are as earthquakes, and are in torment, and are confounded in thunder. Come forth, O Spirit N. in a moment: let thy dwelling-place be empty, apply unto us the secrets of Truth and obey my power. Come forth, visit us in peace, appear unto my eyes; be friendly: Obey the living breath! For I stir thee up in the name of the God of Truth who liveth for ever, Helioren. Obey the living breath, therefore continually unto the end as my thoughts appear to my eyes: therefore be friendly: speaking the secrets of Truth in voice and in understanding.

YE SECOUNDE CONJOURATIOUN

I invoke thee, and move thee, and stir thee up O Spirit N. appear unto my eyes before the circle in the likeness of a man in the names and by the name Iah and Vau, which Adam spake and in the name of God, Agla, which Lot spake: and it was as pleasant deliverers unto him and his house and in the name Ioth which Iacob spake in the voice of the Holy ones who cast him down, and it was also as pleasant deliverers in the anger of his brother and in the name Anaphaxeton, which Aaron spake and it was as the Secret Wisdom and in the name Zabaoth which Mosheh spake, and all things of water were as blood; and in the name Asher Ehyeh Oriston, which Mosheh spake, and all waters were bringing forth creatures who wax strong, which lifted up unto the houses, which destroy all things and in the name of Elion which Mosheh spake, and it was as stones from the firmament of wrath, such as was not in the ages of Time the beginning of the Earth and in the name of Adni, which Mosheh spake and there appeared creatures of earth who destroyed what the big stones did not: and in the name Schema Amathia, which Ioshua invoked, and the Sun remained over ye, O ye hills the seats of Gibeon, and in the names Alpha and Omega which Daniel spake, and destroyed Bel and the Dragon: and in the name Emmanuel which the sons of God sang praises in the midst of the burning plain, and flourished in conquest: and in the name Hagios, and by the Throne of Adni, and in Ischyros, Athanatos, Paracletos: and in O Theos, Ictros, Athanatos. And in these names of secret truth, Agla, On, Tetragrammaton, do I invoke and move thee. And in these names, and all things that are the names of the God of Secret Truth who liveth for ever, the All-Powerful. I invoke and stir thee up, O spirit N. Even by him who spake it was, to whom all creatures are obedient and in the Extreme Justice and Anger of God; and by the veil(?) that is before the glory of God, mighty; and by the creatures of living breath before the Throne whose eyes are east and west; by the fire in the fire of just Glory of the Throne; by the Holy ones of

Heaven; and by the secret wisdom of God, I, exalted in power, stir thee up. Appear before this circle; obey in all things that I say; in the seal Basdathea Baldachia; and in this Name Primeumaton, which Mosheh spake, and the earth was divided, and Korah, Dathan, and Abiram fell in the depth. Therefore obey in all things, O spirit N., obey thy creation. Come thou forth: appear unto my eyes; visit us in peace, be friendly; come forth in the 24th of a moment; obey my power, speaking the secrets of Truth in voice and in understanding!

YE CONSTRAYNTE.

I stir thee up, O spirit N. in all things that are the names of glory and power of God the Great One who is greater than understanding, Adni Ihvh Tzabaoth, come forth in the 24th of a moment, let Thy dwelling-place be empty; apply thyself unto the secret truth and obey my power: appear unto my eyes, visit us in peace, speaking the secrets of truth in voice and understanding. I stir thee up and move thee, O spirit N., in all the names that I have said, and I add these one and six names wherein Solomon, the lord of the secret wisdom, placed yourselves, spirits of wrath, in a vessel, Adonai, Preyai Tetragrammaton, Anaphaxeton Inessenfatoal, Pathtomon and Itemon: appear before this circle; obey in all things my power. And as thou art he that obeys not and comes not I shall be in thy power, O God Most High that liveth for ever, who is the creator of all things in six days Eie, Saraye, and in my power in the name Prieumaton that ruleth over the palaces of heaven, Curse Thee, and destroy thy seat, joy, and power; and I bind thee in the depth of Abaddon, to remain until the day of judgment whose end cannot be. And I bind thee in the fire of sulphur mingled with poison and the seas of fire and sulphur: come forth, therefore, obey my power and appear before this circle. Therefore come forth in the name of the Holy Ones Zabaoth, Adonai, Amioran. Come! for I am Adonai who stir thee up.

YE POTENT INVOCATIOUN OF HYS KYNGE.

O thou great powerful governor Amaimon, who reigneth exalted in the power of the only El above all spirits in the kingdoms of the East, (South, West, North), I invoke and move thee in the name of the true God, and in God whom thou worshippest: and in the seal of thy creation: and in the mighty names of God, Iehevohe Tetragrammaton, who cast thee down from Heaven, thou and the spirits of darkness, and in all the names of the mighty God who is the creator of Heaven and earth, and the dwelling of darkness, and all things and in their power and brightness; and in the name Primeumaton who reigns over the palaces of Heaven. Bring forth, I say, the spirit N.; bring him forth in the 24th of a moment let his dwelling be empty until he visits us in peace, speaking the secrets of truth; until he obey my power and his creation in the power of God, El, who is the Creator and doth dispose of all things, heaven, firmament, earth, and the dwelling of darkness.

YE GENERALL CURSE.

YCLEPT YE SPIRITS' CHAYNE, AGAINST ALL SPIRITS YT REBELLE.

O thou wicket spirit N. that obeyeth not, because I made a law and invoked the names of the glori-

ous and ineffable God of Truth, the creator of all, and thou obeyest not the mighty sounds that I make: therefore I curse thee in the depth of Abaddon to remain until the day of judgment in torment in fire and in sulphur without end, until thou appear before our will and obey my power. Come, therefore, in the 24th of a moment, before the circle in the triangle in this name and by this name of God, Adni, Tzabaoth, Adonai, Amioran. Come! Come! for it is the Lord of Lords Adni, that stirreth thee up.

YE CONJOURATIOUN OF YE FYRE.

I stir thee up, O thou fire, in him who is thy Creator and of all creatures. Torment, burn, destroy the spirit N. always whose end cannot be, I judge thee in judgment and in extreme justice, O spirit N., because thou art he that obeyeth not my power and obeyeth not that law which the Lord God made, and obeyeth not the Mighty Sounds and the Living Breath which I invoke, which I send: Come forth, I, who am the Servant of the Same Most High governor Lord God powerful, Iehovohe, I who am exalted in power and am mighty in his power above ye, O thou who comest not giving obedience and faith to him that liveth and triumpheth. Therefore I say the judgment: I curse thee and destroy the name N. and the seal N., which I have placed in this dwelling of poison, and I burn thee in fire whose end cannot be; and I cast thee down unto the seas of torment, out of which thou shalt not rise until thou come to my eyes: visit me in peace: be friendly before the circle in the △ in the 24th of a moment in the likeness of a man not unto the terror of the sons of men the creatures or all things on the face of the earth. Obey my power like reasoning creatures; obey the living breath, the law which I speak.

YE GRETER CURSE.

Hearken to me, O ye Heavens! O thou Spirit N. because thou art the disobedient one who is wicked and appearest not, speaking the secrets of truth according to the living breath; I, exalted in the power of God, the All-powerful, the center of the circle, powerful God who liveth, whose end cannot be, Iehevohe Tetragrammaton, the only creator of heaven, earth, and dwelling of darkness and all that is in their palaces; who disposeth in secret wisdom of all things in darkness and light: Curse thee and cast thee down and destroy thy seat, joy and power, and I bind thee in the depths of Abaddon, to remain until the day of judgment whose end cannot be, I say, unto the seas of fire and sulphur which I have prepared for the wicked spirits that obey not; the sons of iniquity.

Let the company of heaven curse thee!

Let the sun, moon, all the stars curse thee!

Let the light and all the Holy Ones of Heaven curse thee unto the burning flame that liveth for ever, and unto the torment unspeakable!

And even as thy name and seal, which I have put in this dwelling of poison, shall be in torment among creatures of sulphur and bitter sting, burning in fire of earth, in them Iehevohe and exalted in power in these three names, Tetragrammaton Anaphaxeton, Primeumaton, I cast thee down, O wicked spirit N. unto the seas of fire and sulphur which are prepared for the wicked spirits that obey not, the sons of iniquity, to remain until the day of judgment; let the Mercies of God forget thee; let the face of God forget the face of N. who will not see light: let God forget, I say that shall be the balance of justice over the sons of living breath and death and the world, by fire.

YE ADDRESSE UNTO YE SPIRIT ON HYS COMING.

Behold! I confound thee as thou art he that obeys not! Behold the mysteries of the seal of Solomon which I bring forth unto thy power and presence! Behold the creator, the centre of the circle of the living breath; he that is exalted in the power of God and shall not see unto the terror: he that powerfully invoketh and stirreth thee up unto visible appearance: he, the lord of thy governments whose Name is called Octinomos.

Obey, therefore, my power as a reasoning creature in the name of the Lord.

YE WELCOME UNTO Y^E SPIRIT DYGNYTIE.

I am he that is looking with gladness upon thee, O thou spirit . . . N. beautiful and praiseworthy! with gladness I say, because thou art called in him who is creator of Heaven and earth and the dwelling of darkness, and all things that are in their palaces, and because thou art the servant of obedience. In these the power by which thou art obedient to the living breath, I bind thee to remain visible to our eyes in power and presence as the servant of fealty before the circle until I say "Descend unto thy dwelling" until the living breath of the voice of the Lord is according to the law which shall be given unto thee.

By the seal of the secret wisdom of Solomon thou art called!

Obey the mighty sounds! obey the living breath of the voice of the Lord!

Follows ye charge.

YE LICENSE TO YE SPIRIT Y^T HE MAYE DEPART.

O thou Spirit N. because thou art the servant of fealty and obedience, and because thou art he that obeyeth my power and thy creation; therefore I say Descend unto thy dwelling, obey the law which I have made, without terror to the sons of men, creatures, all things upon the surface of the earth.

Descend therefore I say, and be thou as stewards of Time; come forth in a moment, even as servants that hearken to the voice of the Lord; in the moment in which I invoke thee and stir thee up and move thee in the mysteries of the secret wisdom of the Creator!

Descend unto thy dwelling place in pleasure: let there be the mercies of God upon thee: be friendly in continuing; whose long continuance shall be comforters unto all creatures. Amen.

Additional Commentary

Among the seventy-two spirits catalogued in *The Lesser Key of Solomon*, a select few can be traced, either explicitly or implicitly, to figures found within the canonical and deuterocanonical scriptures. Chief among these is Bael (or Baal), the Canaanite storm and fertility deity repeatedly condemned in the Hebrew Bible as a central figure of idolatry. Baal is referenced in *Judges 2:11*, *1 Kings 18:21*, and *Jeremiah 19:5*, where the Israelites are admonished for turning to foreign gods, often in connection with fertility cults and ritual transgressions.

Asmoday, also rendered Asmodeus, finds his clearest biblical attestation in the *Book of Tobit*, a deuterocanonical text included in Catholic and Orthodox canons. In *Tobit 3:8* and *6:14-17*, Asmodeus appears as the demon responsible for killing seven of Sarah's husbands before their marriages can be consummated. This account secured his role in Jewish demonology as a personification of lust, envy, and destructive obsession.

The figure of Amon also appears in multiple biblical contexts. *2 Kings 21:18-26* names Amon as a historical king of Judah and son of Manasseh. Yet in *Jeremiah 46:25*, a separate "Amon of No" evokes the Egyptian god Amun-Ra, suggesting that the Goetic spirit may conflate or corrupt these identities. The resulting figure in the *Goetia* is likely a syncretic blending of Egyptian solar deification with post-biblical demonological evolution.

Belial presents another compelling transition. Originally a Hebrew term denoting "worthlessness" or "lawlessness" (*Deuteronomy 13:13*, *Judges 19:22*), Belial later develops into a fully personified demon in Second Temple literature. He figures prominently in the *Dead Sea Scrolls* as the adversary of the Sons of Light, and in *2 Corinthians 6:15*, he is rhetorically contrasted with Christ, marking his transition from abstract noun to cosmic antagonist.

Baalberith, or Berith, is referenced in *Judges 8:33* and *9:4* as the "Lord of the Covenant," a deity worshipped in Shechem by the apostate Israelites. Over time, this Canaanite god of treaties and covenants was absorbed into demonological traditions as a corrupter of contracts and a subverter of oaths.

Additional spirits, while lacking biblical attestations, nonetheless bear mythological and folkloric provenance. Paimon, though absent from scripture, may originate in pre-Islamic Arabian folklore; his name likely derives from *al-Qaimun*—"the one who stands" or "keeper." His rulership over hidden knowledge and obedience aligns with jinn-like figures in Islamic tradition. Astaroth, too, is a masculinized version of Astarte or Ashtoreth, the Canaanite goddess condemned in *1 Kings 11:5* and *Judges 2:13*. Her transformation from goddess to male demon exemplifies the Christian impulse to desacralize pagan divinities through inversion and gender corruption.

Other figures like Beleth (or Bileth) may derive from Mesopotamian deities such as Baalat or Belet-Seri, goddesses of death and the underworld, though these connections remain speculative. Furfur, whose name evokes the Latin for "bran," might be a garbled transmission of a weather spirit or rustic demon, while Dantalion, whose function is to influence thoughts and emotions, may descend from medieval angelology or Islamic jinn tales—serving as an esoteric figure of psychospiritual manipulation.

Phenex is clearly drawn from the myth of the phoenix, a Greco-Egyptian bird symbolizing rebirth and resurrection, long integrated into early Christian typology. Bifrons, whose dual gaze mirrors the Roman god Janus Bifrons, governs transitions, memory, and graveyards, embodying liminality. Valefor is sometimes linked to *valetudo* (Latin for "health" or "sickness") and appears as a trickster-spirit or folkloric thief. Gaap, potentially derived from the Arabic *al-Ghaf* ("the hidden"), resembles a jinn functioning as a psychopomp and master of occult knowledge. Zagan, finally, may bear etymological ties to the Hebrew *sagan* ("chief officer"), but more likely emerges as a creative projection of Renaissance magical imagination, concerned with alchemy and the manipulation of form.

In sum, while only a minority of the *Goetia*'s spirits can be firmly situated within the biblical or apocryphal canon, a broader constellation of mythic, folkloric, and linguistic traditions informs their construction. Their origins lie not in any one sacred corpus but in the imaginative syncretism of early modern grimoires, which freely draw upon scripture, legend, and esoteric cosmologies to compose a functioning spiritual taxonomy.

Yet, the borrowing does not stop with the names of spirits. *The Lesser Key of Solomon*, particularly in its *Goetia* section, presents itself as a ritual manual rooted in Solomonic authority, and its literary and theological architecture bears unmistakable parallels to the Hebrew Bible, the New Testament, and various apocryphal writings. These echoes are not superficial but are deeply embedded in the prayers, conjurations, and ritual frameworks throughout the text.

A foundational element of the *Goetia*'s operative system is its reliance on the invocation of divine names. Most notably, it employs the Tetragrammaton (YHVH), Elohim, Adonai, El, and *Ehyeh Asher Ehyeh*—names directly lifted from the Old Testament. The expression "I AM THAT I AM" (*Exodus 3:14*), as well as the phrase "God of Abraham, God of Isaac, and God of Jacob" (*Exodus 3:6*), function in the *Goetia* as formulae to legitimize authority, assert divine ancestry, and place the magician in a covenantal lineage.

The stylistic cadence of the conjurations borrows heavily from the psalms and prophetic books, replicating their use of parallel structure, poetic epithets, and martial imagery. Phrases such as "Who rideth upon the heavens" (*Psalm 68:4*) and "The Lord is a man of war" (*Exodus 15:3*) appear verbatim or in paraphrase, lending the rituals a scriptural solemnity while portraying the magician as a holy combatant against chaos and rebellion.

The inclusion of angelic names—Michael, Gabriel, Raphael, and Uriel—further ties the grimoire to canonical and intertestamental texts. Michael, called a "chief prince" in *Daniel 10:13*, and Gabriel, the divine herald in *Daniel 8:16* and *Luke 1:19*, appear frequently in the conjurations. Raphael plays a central role in *Tobit*, and Uriel, though absent from Protestant scripture, is featured in *2 Esdras 4:1* as Ezra's angelic interlocutor. These angels are not merely symbolic; they function as authorities and witnesses, securing and enforcing the magician's control over infernal spirits.

Moreover, the *Goetia*'s hierarchical taxonomy of spirits—grouping them into kings, dukes, marquises, and so on—mirrors the celestial orders found in *1 Enoch*, where angels and watchers are categorized and judged. The motif of spiritual bondage also resonates with *Revelation 20:1-3*, wherein Satan is bound in chains and sealed in the Abyss, a motif reenacted in the magician's use of sigils, pentacles, and binding prayers.

The "License to Depart," a standard formula used to dismiss spirits after evocation, closes many rituals with an adjuration for peace and nonviolence. This echoes the biblical principle of divine protection in spiritual warfare, as seen in *Job 1:12* and *Luke 10:19*, where power is given over adversarial forces without the loss of divine favor.

The *Ars Notoria*, the final book of the *Lemegeton*, introduces Latin prayers infused with explicitly Christian theology, often invoking the Holy Trinity or citing liturgical formulas reminiscent of medieval sacramentaries. One finds quotations and paraphrases from the *Gospel of John*, particularly *John 1:1* ("In the beginning was the Word"), which serves to sanctify the intellect and align the aspirant with divine wisdom—a ritual gesture that connects magical efficacy to Logos-centered metaphysics.

In conclusion, while the *Lesser Key of Solomon* operates as a manual of ceremonial magic, its structural and theological scaffolding is deeply indebted to both the Hebrew and Christian scriptures, as well as apocryphal and folkloric traditions. Its spirits—some drawn from ancient texts, others from the creative imagination—inhabit a liturgical framework steeped in biblical language, patriarchal formulas, angelic names, and apocalyptic imagery. Far from being a rupture from the religious world it mimics, the *Goetia* reconstitutes that world into a working model of spiritual authority, rendering the magician a priestly figure wielding sacred language to command shadow.

Conclusion: The Lesser Key of Solomon and the Invention of Infernal Order

To conclude our examination of the *Goetia*, it is necessary to step back from the seductive lore of infernal legions and face the document as it truly is: an elegant, inconsistent, often ingenious artifact of syncretic mysticism, psychological projection, and literary creativity. While it claims origin in the wisdom of Solomon, its true genealogy is far more modern, muddled, and meaningful—not despite its errors, but precisely because of them.

The Origins: Post-Solomonic and Preposterously Attributed

The *Lesser Key of Solomon*, or *Lemegeton*, is a 17th-century English compilation masquerading as ancient Hebrew magic. Its structure, divided into five books (with the *Goetia* being the first), reflects post-Renaissance attempts to catalog the supernatural with the same fervor naturalists once reserved for beetles and birds. The claim that Solomon composed these charts of demons, complete with sigils, planetary hours, and magical implements, is not supported by any extant ancient Hebrew, Greek, or Aramaic source. It is a pious fiction—crafted for effect.

That is not to say the system is meaningless. Far from it. But it does not descend from Solomon. It rises from the minds of early modern mystics, alchemists, and clerics—men operating in the shadow of collapsing Christendom, seeking a new order in the ruins of both reason and ritual.

Johann Weyer: Demonology as Early Psychology

Among the key figures behind the Goetia's development is **Johann Weyer**, a Dutch physician and former student of Heinrich Cornelius Agrippa. Weyer's *Pseudomonarchia Daemonum* (1577) is a pivotal precursor text, listing many of the same spirits that appear in the *Goetia*. But Weyer's intent was neither magical nor reverential. He was a medical man with a protective impulse: to expose what he saw as the mass hysteria behind witch trials, and to argue that many so-called possessions were signs of mental illness, not spiritual invasion.

In this sense, Weyer can be seen as a proto-Jungian—mapping not an infernal cosmology, but a shadow psychology. And here lies one of the most fascinating ironies: the *Goetia* borrows heavily from a text designed to discredit the very practices it inspired.

Publishing and the Occult Marketplace: DeLaurence & Co.

By the 19th century, the *Goetia* had become the province of publishers, not prophets. **L.W. de Laurence**, among the most infamous, reissued grimoires with flamboyant flair and sometimes dubious editorial ethics. His publications, printed in Chicago and distributed widely in Africa and the Caribbean, did more than preserve esoteric knowledge—they **commodified** it. They sold dreams of power, lists of ritual objects, and diagrams of supposed spiritual machinery to anyone with a dollar and a hunger for dominion.

The real magic here, one suspects, was marketing. Instructions like "consistency is rewarded" brilliantly shifted the burden of efficacy from text to practitioner. If the rite failed, it was not the system that erred—it was you. A model still widely used today in everything from online coaching to self-help mysticism.

Syncretism and Fabrication

Many have claimed the Goetia is simply a demonization of older pagan gods—Baal, Astaroth, Asmodeus, Amon. While there are echoes of Canaanite, Babylonian, and Hellenic deities among a few of the 72 spirits, most are pure invention: **Latinized names with**

medieval flair, conjured more from imagination and etymological mimicry than from any known pantheon.

This undermines the central conceit of the *Lemegeton*—that Solomon, a Hebrew monarch ruling in the 10th century BCE, somehow trapped spirits that wouldn't exist in any form until 1500 years later. Unless we're to believe Solomon had a crystal ball tuned to post-Reformation England, this notion collapses under the weight of historical absurdity.

Yet, the idea persists—because it is compelling. The narrative of Solomon binding rebellious spirits and locking them beneath temple stones offers a perfect myth: one of absolute control, cosmic justice, and secret knowledge. It's no surprise that such a tale would attract centuries of elaboration.

Archetype and System: The Goetia and the Tarot

There are 72 spirits in the *Goetia*, and 78 cards in the **Tarot**. This is likely not coincidence. Each spirit, like each card, represents an **archetypal force**: a psychological condition, a spiritual quality, a lesson, or a temptation. *Paimon* rules over dignity and secret knowledge. *Dantalion* governs empathy and emotional complexity. *Amon* evokes the duality of loyalty and conflict.

The Tarot and the Goetia are twin systems of symbolic language. One reflects divine cycles, the other maps shadow forces. That magicians now use both in tandem is not anachronism—it's recognition of their **shared symbolic DNA**.

So What Are We Left With?

A system of demons named by a Christian skeptic, edited by occult entrepreneurs, compiled by anonymous scribes centuries after Solomon, and adopted by generations of seekers as a working magical framework. That the system *works* for some practitioners does not prove its ancient pedigree—it proves the mind's ability to assign meaning, to ritualize intent, and to cohere chaos into structure.

If the *Goetia* has power, it is because **we have given it power**—through belief, repetition, fear, and fascination. That is not fraud. That is mythmaking.

But let us also be honest: the Goetia is not a pristine transmission of ancient wisdom. It is a **collage**—a brilliant, chaotic, occasionally exploitative collage of fear, longing, intellect, and projection. Its spirits are not the demons of old religions; they are the demons of human consciousness—named, ordered, and invoked with remarkable consistency.

And as with all powerful myths: once unleashed, they do not return quietly to their cage.

Appendix

1. Bael, listed first among the seventy-two spirits of the *Ars Goetia*, is widely understood to be a demonized form of the ancient deity Baal. The term *baʿal* in Hebrew signifies "lord" or "master," and was commonly used as a title for various Canaanite and Phoenician gods, including Hadad, the storm god worshipped in Ugarit, Tyre, and Sidon. Baal appears frequently in the Hebrew Bible as a rival deity to Yahweh, representing apostasy and idolatry. The prophet Elijah famously confronts the prophets of Baal in a dramatic contest of divine power: "Then the fire of the Lord fell, and consumed the burnt sacrifice... And when all the people saw it, they fell on their faces: and they said, The Lord, he is the God" (1 Kings 18:38–39). Baal worship is also condemned in the time of the Judges: "And the children of Israel did evil in the sight of the Lord, and served Baalim" (Judges 2:11). In the *Lemegeton*, Baal becomes Bael, transformed from a local god into a subdued infernal king under the command of Solomon. He is described as appearing with the heads of a man, a cat, and a toad, and is said to bestow the power of invisibility. This transition reflects a broader demonological pattern in which deities of vanquished or rival religions are recast as fallen entities—part of the ideological framework by which early modern grimoires asserted the supremacy of Christian cosmology over older religious traditions. Bael, in this context, is not merely a demonic being but a spectral echo of a

once-venerated divine name, now refracted through the lens of spiritual opposition and conquest.

2. Agares, the second spirit listed in the *Ars Goetia*, does not appear by name in any canonical or apocryphal biblical text, nor in known pseudepigrapha. Nevertheless, his functions—teaching all languages, causing those who flee to return, and instigating earthquakes—suggest a syncretic character drawn from several mythological and folkloric traditions. His mount, a crocodile, may evoke the Egyptian deity Sobek, who presided over fertility, war, and the Nile. Agares' dominion over speech and movement implies a role akin to that of the angel Penemue in *1 Enoch 8:3*, who taught humanity writing and wisdom. The teaching of languages is a recurrent theme in fallen angel literature, wherein divine knowledge is distributed prematurely to humankind. Additionally, Agares' power to compel fugitives to return evokes angelic or punitive roles in Islamic and biblical judgment narratives, even if no direct parallel exists. Some etymological speculation links his name to the Arabic *al-Aghar* ("the illustrious"), further suggesting a residual echo of the Islamic djinn kings found in grimoires such as the *Shams al-Ma'arif*. The Latin root *agari* (to chase or drive) may also contribute to the name's constructed identity within the Western magical tradition. Though his origins are speculative, Agares represents the enduring magical concept of commanding the terrestrial and linguistic realms—areas once governed by angels and now, through inversion, attributed to infernal princes.

3. Vassago, the third spirit of the *Ars Goetia*, has no known presence in the Hebrew Bible, Christian Apocrypha, or the major pseudepigraphal texts such as the *Books of Enoch* or the *Testament of Solomon*. His name appears to be a neologism, possibly intended to resemble Iberian or Latinate constructions, though no clear linguistic root has been identified. In grimoires, Vassago is described as a spirit of good nature who reveals past and future events and discovers hidden or lost things. This characterization places him within the tradition of prophetic and oracular beings, which includes both biblical figures and classical analogues. While unnamed, a New Testament account references a young woman with "a spirit of divination" (Greek: πνεῦμα πύθωνα, *pneuma pythōna*) who "brought her masters much gain by soothsaying" (Acts 16:16). This spirit, associated with the oracle of Delphi, embodies the Greco-Roman daemon of prophecy. Vassago's functions also parallel the angel Uriel, especially as presented in *2 Esdras* (4 Ezra), where he imparts hidden knowledge about creation and the fate of souls. His association with lost things and esoteric truth may likewise suggest ties to Penemue and other Watchers in Enochian literature, who taught humanity wisdom both beneficial and forbidden. Vassago, then, is best understood as an invented but coherent type within the magical worldview—a benign spirit of revelation who bridges the space between divine insight and necromantic access to unseen realms.

4. Samigina, also listed as Gamigin in variant manuscripts, is the fourth spirit in the *Ars Goetia* and does not appear in any canonical or extracanonical biblical texts. His functions—teaching the liberal arts and retrieving the souls of the dead—align him with spirits traditionally associated with both pedagogy and necromancy. The liberal arts were themselves viewed in medieval cosmology as disciplines of divine origin, and to teach them placed a spirit in the role of a former angelic intermediary. In this respect, Samigina shares a thematic connection with the Watchers of *1 Enoch 8*, particularly Penemue and Kasdeja, who taught writing, astrology, and sorcery to humanity. His command over the "aerial dead" evokes the scene in *1 Samuel 28*, where the Witch of Endor summons the spirit of Samuel at Saul's request—an act explicitly condemned by biblical law: "There shall not be found among you... a consulter with familiar spirits, or a wizard, or a necromancer" (Deuteronomy 18:10-11). The aerial nature of the souls Samigina governs also finds resonance in Platonic and Gnostic thought, where spirits between incarnation and ascent are imagined to inhabit intermediary regions of air or ether. Gnostic scriptures such as the *Apocryphon of John* describe soul realms that precede final judgment, populated by archons and spirits whose roles include both assistance and hindrance. The name "Gamigin" may be a magical corruption or adaptation of names like "Gamaliel," known in Kabbalistic texts as a governing angelic force. However, unlike the celestial Gamaliel, Samigina operates from the

infernal register, guiding souls not toward salvation, but toward revelation of hidden truths through liminal and forbidden channels.

5. Marbas, the fifth spirit, does not occur in the Bible, nor is there a corresponding figure in the major mythological corpora of antiquity. Despite this, his characteristics resonate with deeply embedded archetypes within Judeo-Christian and ancient Near Eastern thought. Marbas is described as taking the form of a great lion, and possessing the powers of healing or causing disease, transforming people's shapes, and revealing hidden truths. The lion is an ambivalent symbol in biblical literature. On the one hand, it is the emblem of divine authority and messianic kingship—as in the "Lion of Judah" (Revelation 5:5). On the other, it figures prominently in apocalyptic and destructive imagery, as in the bestial visions of Daniel 7. Marbas's dual capacity to heal and to harm finds precedent in both angelic and demonic figures: the archangel Raphael, in the *Book of Tobit*, heals Tobit and binds the demon Asmodeus (Tobit 8:3); whereas Satan smites Job with boils in *Job 2:7*. The ability to shape-shift recalls the traditions of ancient witches and gods—Proteus, Circe, and even some Watchers—who mastered the mutable powers of form. His reputed knowledge of mechanical arts may suggest an echo of Tubal-Cain, the first artificer in *Genesis 4:22*, whose lineage was often conflated with the fallen angels in later mystical and magical literature. Though his name may derive from "Barbas"—a term associated with beards or wisdom—the transformation into "Marbas" gives the name an

exotic, perhaps Mesopotamian quality. Whether invented or refracted through oral traditions, Marbas occupies the liminal space between healing spirit and technical daemon, making him an agent of esoteric craftsmanship and corporeal transformation.

6. Valefor, the sixth spirit of the *Ars Goetia*, is absent from the Bible and from all major theological or mythological corpora of antiquity. Described as a duke who appears in the form of a lion with the head of a man, Valefor is credited with fostering theft and dishonesty, often tempting magicians to steal while simultaneously granting them the illusion of loyal companionship. His name is likely a Latinized construction, possibly from *valeo* ("to be strong") and *fero* ("to bring or carry"), implying a bearer of strength—or, perhaps more ironically, a bringer of ruin. His role as a familiar spirit who becomes a false friend mirrors the function of certain djinn in Islamic lore, who serve magicians but ultimately betray them. Similarly, in Christian tradition, Satan is described as one who comes "to steal, and to kill, and to destroy" (John 10:10), and Judas Iscariot embodies the archetype of the trusted companion who betrays. Valefor's animal-headed form also recalls the gods of Egypt, such as Anubis or Thoth, and later occult icons like Baphomet, whose fusion of human and beast signifies hidden knowledge or inversion. Although no scriptural basis exists for his name or function, Valefor's portrayal serves as a cautionary figure in ritual magic—warning of the seductive charm of unlawful

gain and the moral cost of deception cloaked in loyalty.

7. Amon, the seventh spirit, is one of the few Goetic names that has clear attestation in the Bible, though not in a demonic sense. Two primary references exist. First, Amon is the son of Manasseh and a king of Judah, who "did that which was evil in the sight of the Lord" and was assassinated by his own servants (2 Kings 21:19-23; 2 Chronicles 33:21-24). Second, the Hebrew term *No-Amon* (נֹא אָמוֹן), translated as "Populous No," refers to the Egyptian city of Thebes, where the god Amun (or Amon) was worshipped. This deity, often syncretized as Amun-Ra, was the principal god of Thebes, associated with kingship, fertility, and hidden power. The prophet Nahum denounces the city: "Art thou better than populous No, that was situate among the rivers… Yet was she carried away, she went into captivity" (Nahum 3:8-10). The Goetic Amon appears to conflate both figures—the biblical king and the Egyptian god—into a single spirit, reflecting the demonological tendency to collapse pagan theonyms into infernal identities. Amon is said to reconcile feuding parties, stir up love, and reveal past and future, thereby assuming roles linked to both divine mediation and romantic manipulation. His duality mirrors the complex legacy of Amun as a creator and unifier, as well as the king of Judah whose legacy is marked by apostasy. The name Amon is sometimes conflated with Amaimon, one of the four cardinal kings of Hell in later grimoires. In this regard, Amon exemplifies the demonological habit of transposing

foreign deities into the demon host, recasting religious alterity as spiritual rebellion.
8. Barbatos, the eighth spirit, finds no mention in the Bible or related literature, though his characteristics resonate with classical and folkloric themes. He is described as appearing in the form of a horned archer surrounded by a harmonious entourage, capable of revealing hidden treasures, reconciling disputes, and speaking the language of animals. His name likely derives from the Latin *barbatus*, meaning "bearded," possibly invoking an image of ancient wisdom. Barbatos's abilities to mediate between animals and humans align him with figures such as Orpheus, who in classical mythology charmed animals with music, or with Solomon, who, according to later Islamic tradition, understood the language of birds (cf. Qur'an 27:16). The power to reveal hidden treasure places him within the tradition of chthonic deities like Pluto or psychopomps such as Hermes and Thoth, both of whom govern hidden realms. His musical and forest-bound nature may also echo the Green Man of medieval lore, Pan of Greek mythology, or elvish kings of Germanic tales. The combination of nobility, pastoral harmony, and hidden knowledge renders Barbatos a druidic or shamanic figure within the infernal hierarchy. Though absent from scripture, he encapsulates a romantic vision of the daemon as wise wild man—one whose allegiance is neither fully to darkness nor to light, but to a deeper rhythm of nature and its unseen laws.
9. Paimon, the ninth spirit and one of the most celebrated in modern occult circles, is notably

absent from biblical and traditional scriptural sources. His name has been variously theorized to derive from Persian *Payman* (covenant) or Arabic constructions resembling the djinn lore of the Middle East, though no exact antecedent has been confirmed. Paimon is said to appear with great pomp, preceded by musicians and accompanied by a retinue, and manifests in a crowned and effeminate form. His powers include revealing hidden knowledge, teaching arts and sciences, and commanding obedient legions. These traits place him in the line of angelic scribes such as Raziel and Metatron in Jewish mysticism, or even the androgynous daemons of Gnostic mythologies. His command of science and art suggests a Promethean archetype—one who bestows divine secrets at a cost. Some scholars see in his effeminacy and nobility echoes of the solar deity Apollo, or of Thoth, the Egyptian scribe-god. The pomp of his arrival evokes descriptions of courtly procession and divine hierophany. While lacking any biblical citation, Paimon has come to symbolize infernal enlightenment: knowledge granted not through grace, but through pact and ritual. His recent depiction in popular culture, particularly the 2018 film *Hereditary*, has elevated his profile, reinforcing his dual identity as both teacher and test.

10. Buer, the tenth spirit, has no known scriptural basis and is not associated with any mythological deity of antiquity. He is described in magical texts as possessing the form of a multi-legged wheel or lion-centaur, a symbol that may evoke the vision of the Ophanim in *Ezekiel 1:15–21*, where wheels intersect

and move with spiritual force. Buer teaches natural and moral philosophy, the virtues of herbs, and the healing of both human and animal ailments. These attributes suggest alignment with classical figures such as Asclepius, the Greek god of healing, or Chiron, the wise centaur who instructed heroes. His gift of familiar spirits also connects him to the tradition of magical companions, prominent in both Solomonic and folk magic, whereby spirits assist the magician in physical and spiritual tasks. Though his name lacks clear etymology, Buer functions as a daemon of temperance and clarity, a rational force within the infernal court. His focus on health and ethics marks him as one of the few Goetic spirits whose domain is primarily beneficent, highlighting the ambivalent nature of magic—capable of healing as well as harm, depending on the hand that wields it.

11. Gusion, the eleventh spirit of the *Ars Goetia*, is not found in the canon of scripture, nor in the known apocryphal or pseudepigraphal works. Nevertheless, his described abilities—reconciling enemies, answering questions about the past, present, and future, and granting honor and dignity—place him among the ranks of daemonic counselors whose roles mirror that of the wise interpreter or prophet. Although there is no clear etymology for the name "Gusion," speculative linguistic roots have been proposed, including Latin *gusto* ("to taste" or "to perceive"), implying discernment or judgment. His function evokes the biblical image of wise judges and mediators, such as Solomon, whose decisions reconciled disputes, or

the prophetic role of Daniel, who interpreted dreams and revealed divine mysteries. In *1 Enoch* and associated angelology, similar roles are given to the Watchers and archangels—especially Raphael and Uriel—who provide insight into divine law and human fate. Gusion's appearance as a "foreign man" may suggest the motif of the outsider bearing truth, as seen in the figure of Melchizedek (Genesis 14), or the magi who discerned the birth of Christ (Matthew 2). Though he holds no biblical pedigree, Gusion's persona integrates the qualities of prophet, diplomat, and philosopher, rendering him a spirit of governance, persuasion, and temporal knowledge.

12. Sitri, the twelfth spirit in the Goetic hierarchy, has no attestation in biblical or mythological sources under any known variation of his name. He is said to incite love and lust between men and women, and to cause individuals to reveal their secret desires or affections. In his form, Sitri is described as having the face of a leopard with the wings of a griffon, though he appears as a beautiful man when commanded by the magician. This composite form—half beast, half seductive human—places Sitri within a broad symbolic category of spirits of passion, lust, and emotional entanglement. In biblical terms, such entities are not personified but often condemned in principle; the *Book of Proverbs* warns repeatedly against the seductress and the dangers of unrestrained desire: "With her much fair speech she caused him to yield... he goeth after her straightway, as an ox goeth to the slaughter" (Proverbs 7:21-22). Sitri's actions also

recall the demon Asmodeus in the *Book of Tobit*, who slays the husbands of Sarah out of jealousy, representing the destructive side of erotic power. The ability to unmask hearts and manipulate romantic energies draws on an archetype that spans cultures: from Eros and Aphrodite in Greek mythology to the djinn of Islamic lore, many spirits were invoked or feared for their control over love. Sitri, then, represents the volatile intersection of beauty and danger—a daemon of desire who reveals as much as he ensnares, and whose gifts may illuminate hidden truth or provoke ruin.

13. Beleth, the thirteenth spirit, occupies a prominent role in early grimoires and is described as a powerful and terrible king who must be approached with great caution. Though his name bears superficial resemblance to "Belial," a term used in the Bible to signify worthlessness or lawlessness—"What concord hath Christ with Belial?" (2 Corinthians 6:15)—there is no evidence that Beleth is derived directly from that source. Instead, he appears to be an invented figure or a composite of several archetypes. Beleth is said to arrive with a great parade of trumpets and riders, seated on a pale horse, which evokes the apocalyptic vision of the fourth horseman in Revelation: "And I looked, and behold a pale horse: and his name that sat on him was Death" (Revelation 6:8). He is invoked in matters of love, particularly the creation of passion or reconciliation between lovers, though he is feared for his wrathful presence and must be compelled with specific ritual discipline. Beleth's portrayal combines both regal majesty and erotic command,

aligning him symbolically with spirits such as Cupid or Eros, who inspire longing, but also with angelic figures who terrify upon arrival. The magician's requirement to maintain composure and command in his presence underscores the ritual principle that only mastery over self and spirit alike grants safe access to divine or infernal powers. Beleth thus exemplifies the daemon of awe and desire—a sovereign whose domain is the perilous terrain of love made law.

14. Leraje, also spelled Leraikha in some manuscripts, is the fourteenth spirit listed in the *Ars Goetia* and does not appear in the Bible or in recognized mythological canons. He is described as a handsome archer clad in green who carries a bow and quiver and is capable of inciting conflict, particularly among armies. The wounds caused by his arrows are said to become infected, a detail which may have symbolic or ritual significance. Leraje's persona reflects the archetype of the martial daemon—one who governs war, but not through brute force. His association with precision, archery, and putrefaction suggests a metaphysical commentary on the hidden causes of conflict and the slow decay of peace. In classical mythology, similar figures include Apollo, who both heals and spreads plague through arrows, and Ares, the god of war, who represents discord and passion. The idea of wounds that corrupt over time may also reflect moral decay or the unseen consequences of pride and ambition, themes explored throughout the Wisdom literature of the Bible. Though not mentioned in scripture, Leraje echoes the

iconography of silent, elegant warfare—a daemon of duel, not massacre; of poisoned honor, not chaos. His presence in ritual magic would likely be invoked for influence over battle, rivalry, or sabotage, and he may be viewed as a spiritual agent of conflict whose harm lies not in strength but in infection of the will.

15. Eligos, the fifteenth spirit, does not appear in scripture but is a fully developed figure within the demonological imagination of the Renaissance. He is portrayed as a duke who rides a great steed, bearing a lance, standard, and scepter. His powers include revealing hidden causes of warfare, discerning the intentions of enemies, and securing the favor of nobles and dignitaries. Eligos thus occupies the role of a martial tactician and political manipulator, akin to the angelic or mythic archetypes of Hermes, Athena, or Michael, all of whom combine intelligence with force. The ability to divine secret plans and to forecast conflict suggests a parallel with the prophetic seers of the Old Testament, such as Elisha or Daniel, who exposed the counsels of kings. While not malicious per se, Eligos represents the strategic intellect in service of power—an infernal advisor who governs both diplomacy and destruction. His seductive appearance and ability to incite love also align him with spirits like Amon or Sitri, whose dominion straddles desire and dominion. In the magician's cosmology, Eligos would be summoned not for brute conquest but for victories that depend on insight, charisma, and manipulation. He is the spirit of calculated war—the daemon behind the throne whose wisdom is as dangerous as his weapons.

16. Zepar, the sixteenth spirit of the *Ars Goetia*, is not found in any canonical scripture or apocryphal literature, yet his role within the demonological corpus is clear: he governs lust, particularly between men and women, and is known to influence the heart to love or desire while simultaneously rendering women barren. The paradox of attraction coupled with infertility reflects an ambivalent spiritual symbolism, where erotic compulsion is divorced from generative outcome. Though the etymology of his name is uncertain, Zepar's characterization aligns with classical figures such as Eros or Asmodeus—the latter appearing in the *Book of Tobit* as a demon of lust who prevents Sarah from consummating any marriage (*Tobit 3:8*). In visual depictions, Zepar is often clothed in red, the color of Mars and symbolic of passion, blood, and conflict. The martial aspect of his attire suggests that his domain is not merely romantic but also strategic—love weaponized for control, diversion, or manipulation. He is a figure of enchantment rather than harmony, driving desire to its breaking point without fulfillment. In this, Zepar embodies the inversion of divine love into obsession, promising union while sowing disjunction, and thereby representing the dangers of unchecked carnal will within the magician's spiritual practice.

17. Botis, the seventeenth spirit in the hierarchy, does not appear in the Bible nor in known classical mythology. Nevertheless, his symbolic features—most notably his transformation from a viper into a human with large teeth and horns—invoke traditional motifs of revelation, deception, and the

duality of wisdom. He is said to speak truthfully about the past, present, and future, to reconcile friends and foes, and to possess a blunt and forceful manner. The viper form evokes the serpent of Genesis, who offered forbidden knowledge, and whose role in the Fall made the snake a potent symbol of both deceit and illumination: "Now the serpent was more subtil than any beast of the field…" (Genesis 3:1). The ability to resolve disputes links Botis to other spirits of reconciliation, such as Amon and Gusion, while the emphasis on his fearsome and animalistic visage implies that truth, when unfiltered, may appear monstrous. The horns may symbolize spiritual authority or dual perception, as in the horned Moses of medieval iconography. Botis's function as both revealer and peacemaker places him within the liminal space of the truth-teller who speaks what others fear to hear. He is not a spirit of comfort, but of confrontation, embodying the raw and often painful wisdom that precedes healing or resolution.

18. Bathin, the eighteenth spirit, appears in no biblical text and seems to be a wholly constructed figure within the Renaissance grimoire tradition. Described as a serpentine man riding a pale horse, Bathin commands knowledge of herbs, stones, and the properties of natural substances, and is said to transport people and goods swiftly from place to place. His serpentine tail evokes associations with hidden wisdom and arcane power, while the pale horse upon which he rides may allude to the apocalyptic steed in *Revelation 6:8*: "And I looked, and behold a pale horse: and his name that sat on

him was Death." However, Bathin is not a figure of death, but of hidden passage—both physical and metaphysical. His dominion over herbal and mineral knowledge links him with ancient figures like Hermes Trismegistus and Asclepius, who were believed to hold the secrets of nature's healing and transformative powers. His association with swift movement may also point to roles akin to Mercury or Raphael, both of whom serve as divine guides across physical and spiritual terrain. In magical practice, Bathin likely represents the spirit of arcane geography and occult medicine, one who governs the boundaries between realms and facilitates the transition from ignorance to esoteric mastery.

19. Saleos, the nineteenth spirit, is another figure without scriptural precedent, but whose attributes suggest a unique character within the Goetic pantheon. He is often depicted as a soldier riding a crocodile and wearing a crown, combining martial bearing with regal tranquility. Unlike other spirits of love and lust, Saleos is said to promote peace and affection genuinely, encouraging romantic fidelity and emotional healing. This distinguishes him from entities like Zepar or Sitri, whose influence may produce chaos or obsession. The crocodile mount evokes the Egyptian deity Sobek, who was both a god of warfare and fertility—a paradoxical figure of aggression and generative force. Saleos's dual identity as both warrior and reconciler underscores the notion that true love often requires courage, restraint, and strength. While his name bears no identifiable linguistic origin, his role echoes the harmonizing spirits found across magical

traditions—those invoked not to conquer others, but to mend hearts and repair trust. In ceremonial magic, Saleos would be summoned not for seduction or manipulation, but for establishing bonds rooted in sincerity and loyalty. He is the daemon of quiet strength, whose power lies not in force, but in the capacity to bring calm where conflict once reigned.

20. Purson, the twentieth spirit, is a king among the Goetic ranks and is described as a man with a lion's face, riding a bear and sounding a trumpet. He holds a viper in his hand and is attended by hosts of spirits. His abilities include discovering hidden treasures, revealing past and future, and communicating with the spirits of the dead. Though there is no direct reference to Purson in the Bible, his symbolic elements suggest a synthesis of various mythic and esoteric motifs. The lion face aligns him with solar and regal imagery, reminiscent of the "Lion of Judah" (Revelation 5:5), while the bear mount suggests primal strength and the wilderness. The trumpet is a common biblical symbol of divine proclamation or judgment, used repeatedly in the apocalyptic vision of *Revelation* chapters 8 through 11. The viper, again, recalls serpentine knowledge, secrecy, and potential danger. In magical contexts, Purson resembles both Hermes Psychopompos, the guide of souls, and Thoth, who governs sacred knowledge and the underworld. His ability to speak truthfully about both divine and earthly matters suggests a bridge between planes of existence. Though his name may be a corruption of "person" or "persona"—

implying a mask or dual nature—Purson functions as a daemonic regent of revelation, one who grants insight not only into worldly affairs but into the arcane mechanisms of fate and fortune.

21. Marax, also spelled Morax in some sources, is the twenty-first spirit and is absent from biblical or classical mythology under any known form. He is described as appearing in the form of a bull with the face of a man, commanding thirty legions and instructing in astronomy and the liberal sciences. He also imparts knowledge of herbs and precious stones, and gives familiars to the magician. The image of a bull-headed teacher suggests a symbolic fusion of brute strength and intellectual authority, a figure both beastly and wise. This juxtaposition may recall the Apis bull of Egyptian religion, a sacred animal associated with Ptah and Osiris, or the Minotaur of Greek myth—both liminal creatures that mark the boundary between the rational and the monstrous. Marax's role as an instructor of natural and celestial knowledge situates him in the lineage of the Watchers of *1 Enoch 8*, who descended to earth and taught forbidden arts to humankind. He shares thematic ground with Thoth, Hermes Trismegistus, and Enoch himself— each a transmitter of sacred science. Though the name Marax has no secure etymology, its phonetic gravity and Latin resonance enhance the figure's association with hidden knowledge. The gifting of familiars also links him to the witchcraft traditions of early modern Europe, where animal spirits served as magical companions. Marax thus functions as a daemonic professor, a mediator between terrestrial

and astral wisdom whose instruction is precise, potent, and perilously illuminating.

22. Ipos, the twenty-second spirit, is not named in scripture or ancient myth, though his attributes clearly derive from composite archetypes. He is described as appearing with the body of a lion, the feet of a goose, and the head of a hare, and carries a fiery sword. His powers include revealing past and future, bestowing wit and courage, and improving the reputation of those he favors. The animal features of Ipos are emblematic rather than grotesque: the lion evokes power and majesty, the goose vigilance and fidelity, the hare speed and cleverness. Each animal contributes to a symbolic vocabulary of instinctual virtue elevated through daemonic agency. His fiery sword recalls the cherubim who guard Eden in *Genesis 3:24*: "He placed at the east of the garden of Eden Cherubims, and a flaming sword which turned every way, to keep the way of the tree of life." Ipos's role in enhancing courage and renown suggests a function similar to the spirits who assisted warriors, kings, and poets across ancient traditions. The ability to foretell events places him again within the line of the prophetic daemons, yet his gift of charisma implies that he shapes not only what is known, but how one is known. Ipos is thus a daemon of fame and foresight, blending symbolic animal virtues into a singular presence who confers both vision and the gravitas to act upon it.

23. Aim, sometimes rendered as Aym or Haborym in variant texts, is the twenty-third spirit in the Goetic hierarchy and is without precedent in biblical

literature. He appears with three heads—those of a serpent, a man, and a cat—and rides upon a viper while carrying a firebrand with which he sets cities and fortresses ablaze. Aim governs destruction, cleverness, and manipulation, suggesting a dual role as both an incendiary force and a cunning agent of change. The serpent is emblematic of hidden knowledge and danger, the man of reason, and the cat of stealth and independence. The number three in his form may indicate awareness across multiple domains—spiritual, intellectual, and instinctual. The act of setting fire is a recurrent biblical metaphor for divine judgment and cleansing: "The Lord shall judge his people... for our God is a consuming fire" (Hebrews 10:30-31). Yet in Aim's case, fire is not redemptive but anarchic, used to unravel order. His name, possibly a pun on the English "aim," suggests targeted destruction—chaos directed with intent. There may also be an echo of the Hebrew *harab* (חרב), meaning to destroy, though the connection is speculative. In magical terms, Aim represents a force of catalytic upheaval: not malevolent for its own sake, but necessary for transformation, revelation, or revenge. He is the daemon of fire not as element, but as event.

24. Naberius, the twenty-fourth spirit, is commonly associated with the Greek Kerberos (Latin Cerberus), the three-headed hound who guards the underworld. Although not mentioned in the Bible, his attributes—eloquence, restoration of lost honor, and knowledge of the arts and rhetoric—link him with classical daemons of speech and cunning. He is said to appear in the form of a black crane or crow,

speaking with a hoarse voice. In various symbolic systems, the crow represents watchfulness, communication, and boundary-crossing—qualities often attributed to Hermes or Odin, both of whom preside over knowledge and language. The voice of Naberius is rough, perhaps reflecting the hard-won nature of truth, or the dissonance between outer form and inner content. His ability to restore dignity and favor resonates with the role of the intercessor or advocate; his speech is not ornamental, but instrumental, correcting reputation and reshaping perception. The association with Cerberus places him at a threshold: not simply between life and death, but between dishonor and repute, silence and declaration. In magical operations, Naberius is a spirit of self-mastery, of persuasive clarity, and of power regained through eloquence. Though born of infernal imagination, he moves with the authority of a legal or philosophical daemon—one who governs the realm of the spoken word, and the consequences it carries.

25. Glasya-Labolas, the twenty-fifth spirit, has no known antecedent in scripture, though his characteristics draw heavily from classical and folkloric models of war, cunning, and revelation. He is said to appear as a winged dog and to teach the art of murder and bloodshed, as well as invisibility, rhetoric, and the knowledge of all things past and future. The contradiction inherent in his nature—bringer of both wisdom and violence—is central to his identity. He may be compared to figures such as Ares, the Greek god of war, or Azazel, the fallen angel of *1 Enoch* who revealed the arts of warfare to

humanity. The name "Glasya" may echo *gladius* (sword) in Latin, while "Labolas" may derive from *labes* (ruin or downfall), thus forming a compound that signals both power and peril. In his capacity to make one invisible, he invokes the powers of deception and concealment, themes deeply embedded in both magical and theological traditions. His knowledge of past and future places him among the oracular spirits, yet his patronage of murder and treachery makes his wisdom subversive rather than redemptive. Glasya-Labolas is thus a daemon of glory through bloodshed, enlightenment through destruction, and honor through infamy. His gifts are seductive but grave, reminding the magician that power, once invoked, may exact a price as terrible as the truths it reveals.

26. Bune, the twenty-sixth spirit, is presented as a duke who appears in the form of a three-headed dragon, speaking with a deep and resonant voice. He commands legions and is said to move the dead, enrich individuals, grant eloquence, and reveal hidden knowledge, particularly concerning burial places and ancestral spirits. Though he does not appear in the Bible, Bune's necromantic abilities recall scriptural prohibitions against such practices: "Regard not them that have familiar spirits, neither seek after wizards, to be defiled by them" (Leviticus 19:31). The association with the dead and with treasure—material and spiritual—links him to chthonic figures like Hades, Osiris, or Mictlantecuhtli, all of whom preside over the underworld and are keepers of arcane wealth. The connection between death and wisdom is deeply

embedded in esoteric traditions, where the grave is seen as the threshold of higher mysteries. His name may derive from the Hebrew *ben* (son) or *bōnēh* (builder), subtly implying lineage or foundation. In magical operation, Bune is invoked not merely for material gain but for ancestral insight, oration, and the recovery of things buried—whether in earth or in memory. His power is not inherently malevolent, but his gifts come through corridors that few are prepared to walk without consequence.

27. Ronove, the twenty-seventh spirit, appears as a monster carrying a staff and is described as a marquis and earl who teaches languages and rhetoric, grants favor from both allies and enemies, and endows persuasive speech. Though not found in scripture, Ronove's role as a linguistic mediator aligns him with spirits of communication such as Hermes, Thoth, and even the Logos tradition in Christian mysticism. The ability to influence both friends and foes recalls the biblical principle that "A soft answer turneth away wrath: but grievous words stir up anger" (Proverbs 15:1), suggesting a daemonic mastery of the subtleties of tone, phrase, and timing. His name may originate from the Hebrew root *ranan* (רָנַן), meaning to sing or shout with joy, indicating his dominion over vocal expression. Ronove is not a brute persuader but an architect of words, skilled in the calibration of voice to intent. His function as a spirit of diplomacy renders him invaluable in courtly and magical contexts where influence must be exerted with grace rather than coercion. As a figure of both

artistry and advantage, Ronove exemplifies the spirit who confers mastery over one's tongue—the instrument by which favor, alliance, or downfall may be sealed.

28. Berith, the twenty-eighth spirit, is one of the few Goetic entities whose name is attested in the Bible, albeit not in demonic form. In *Judges 8:33* and *9:4*, Baal-Berith is named as a Canaanite deity—"the lord of the covenant"—whose worship marks the apostasy of Israel after Gideon's death. The name derives from the Hebrew *berith* (בְּרִית), meaning covenant or pact, and in its original context may have signified a deity who presided over treaties or binding agreements. In the Goetia, Berith is said to appear in a red vestment, riding a red horse, and speaks in a refined tone. He possesses the power to transmute metals, answer questions truthfully—if compelled—and grant dignities. His crimson symbolism and association with alchemy suggest a corruption of divine covenant into sorcerous pact, reflecting the grimoires' tendency to reinterpret ancient gods as infernal deceivers. Later traditions, including the *Dictionnaire Infernal*, present Berith as a demon of blasphemy, pride, and false prophecy, traits that directly invert the covenantal fidelity implied in his original name. In magical practice, he is approached with caution, as he is reputed to lie unless properly constrained. Berith is a daemon of inversion—once a god of solemn oath, now a prince of falsehood, warning that the binding word, once profaned, can serve either light or ruin.

29. Astaroth, the twenty-ninth spirit, is another figure with biblical ancestry. He is the demonic

transformation of the goddess Ashtoreth, named in *1 Kings 11:5* as a foreign deity whom Solomon himself worshipped in his later years: "For Solomon went after Ashtoreth the goddess of the Zidonians." Ashtoreth, identified with the Phoenician Astarte and the Babylonian Ishtar, was a goddess of fertility, sexuality, and war. In the Goetia, Astaroth is a male spirit who appears as an angel riding a dragon, carrying a viper, and speaking of the Fall of the angels. His knowledge encompasses past, present, and future, and he is known to reveal the secrets of the divine. The inversion from female deity to male demon encapsulates the demonological pattern of casting powerful foreign gods into infernal roles, especially when those gods stood in contrast to Yahwistic monotheism. The presence of the viper in his hand and his appearance atop a dragon reinforce his role as a bearer of forbidden wisdom—symbolically dangerous but rich in insight. In magical ritual, Astaroth is both feared and respected, often invoked for deep metaphysical questions or insight into the angelic rebellion. His speech is intoxicating, and he is said to tempt the magician with knowledge that leads to pride. He is the philosopher-demon, a vestige of divine beauty and celestial memory now entombed in the rhetoric of rebellion.

30. Forneus, the thirtieth spirit, is a marquis who appears in the form of a great sea monster and commands twenty-nine legions. He teaches rhetoric, languages, and brings favor with both enemies and allies. His name suggests a marine origin, possibly derived from the

Latin *fornus* or *furnus* (oven or furnace), but more likely linked conceptually to *Forneus* as a watery force—a daemonic intelligence of the deep. Though absent from scripture, the image of the sea monster evokes the Leviathan of *Job 41*, a fearsome creature whose power is a metaphor for the unknowable might of God: "Canst thou draw out Leviathan with an hook? or his tongue with a cord which thou lettest down?" (Job 41:1). Forneus, unlike Leviathan, is cooperative and instructive, but retains the association with deep waters—symbolically the subconscious, the unknown, and the liminal space between intellect and mystery. His dominion over reputation and rhetorical ability renders him a useful spirit for those navigating courtly or political systems, and his power to reconcile enemies suggests an underlying affinity with diplomacy rather than destruction. In the magician's cosmology, Forneus may be seen as a daemon of deep persuasion—one who emerges from hidden places to shift perception, language, and alliance.

31. Foras, the thirty-first spirit, is described as a mighty president who appears in the form of a strong man. He possesses knowledge of herbs and precious stones, teaches logic and ethics, and grants invisibility, long life, wit, eloquence, and the power to discover lost things or hidden treasures. Though he does not appear in scripture, Foras echoes the image of the wise sage or philosopher, a figure prevalent across biblical and Hellenistic traditions. His dominion over healing and material substances aligns him with archetypal teachers of sacred knowledge such as Hermes Trismegistus or Enoch,

the latter of whom was "translated that he should not see death" (Hebrews 11:5) and is associated in later mystical traditions with esoteric sciences. Foras's gifts also recall Solomon himself, who requested wisdom above all things and received insight into "trees, from the cedar tree that is in Lebanon even unto the hyssop that springeth out of the wall" (1 Kings 4:33). The name Foras may be a corruption of *Phoros*, the Greek for "bearer," possibly implying the bearer of knowledge or light. As a magician's ally, Foras serves as a benefic daemon of clarity and concealment—granting wisdom that protects rather than corrupts, and lengthening life not through magic alone, but through the philosophical temperance he imparts.

32. Asmoday, also known as Asmodeus, is the thirty-second spirit and one of the most notorious demons in the Goetic tradition. He appears with three heads—one of a bull, one of a man, and one of a ram—riding a dragon and bearing a spear. In the *Book of Tobit*, Asmodeus is explicitly named as the demon who slays the seven husbands of Sarah before they can consummate their marriages: "Asmodeus the evil spirit had slain them before they had lain with her" (Tobit 3:8). This biblical citation places him firmly within the tradition of lust and jealous wrath. In later Jewish lore, Asmodeus is known as the king of demons and is often depicted as cunning, learned, and licentious. His Goetic attributes include teaching arithmetic, astronomy, geometry, and all handicrafts, as well as granting invisibility and the favor of kings. The duality in his nature—both destroyer of intimacy and teacher of

refined sciences—reflects the complex conception of spirits in post-biblical demonology. His association with lust is also mirrored in the medieval concept of the seven deadly sins, wherein Asmodeus is commonly linked to lechery or envy. In magical practice, he is treated with extreme caution, as he is said to be proud and difficult to control. Yet his gifts are substantial, offering mastery in both intellectual and sensual domains. Asmoday represents the danger of unchecked genius: brilliant, passionate, and prone to excess.

33. Gaap, the thirty-third spirit, is a president and prince who appears when the sun is in a southern sign and comes with a large entourage. He is said to teach philosophy and the liberal sciences, cause love or hatred, render people insensible, transport individuals across great distances, and instruct on the mysteries of the human soul. While he does not appear in the biblical canon, his role evokes themes found in apocryphal texts and esoteric traditions. His ability to transport and his dominion over love and hatred suggest a spirit that operates in the realm of influence and psychic manipulation—functions associated with both the djinn of Islamic lore and the Watchers of *1 Enoch*, who altered the emotional and social dynamics of early humanity. The name Gaap has no clear etymology, though some speculate a link to the Arabic *qāʾib* (غائب), meaning "absent" or "hidden," possibly signifying a spirit of the invisible realms. His control over the affections of others and his access to hidden knowledge render him a powerful and dangerous ally. In ceremonial magic, Gaap would be invoked

to alter perception, distance, and desire—acts that are as potent politically and emotionally as they are physically. He is a daemon of liminality, situated between intellect and influence, philosophy and passion.

34. Furfur, the thirty-fourth spirit, is a count who appears first as a hart or winged deer and only assumes human form when compelled into a magic triangle. He speaks in a rough voice and is a known liar unless constrained. Yet, once bound, he speaks truly and reveals divine secrets, the causes of storms, and the nature of love between individuals. His capacity to incite tempests suggests alignment with elemental spirits or storm deities of old, while his function in revealing love places him in proximity to spirits like Sitri or Zepar, albeit with a celestial orientation. His dual nature—untruthful when unbound, but a revealer of divine matters when constrained—embodies the magical tension between deception and revelation. The hart form may symbolize elusiveness or purity, while the act of transformation into man implies the necessity of ritual control over chaotic or misleading forces. In scriptural terms, storms are often the voice or wrath of God, as in Psalm 29: "The voice of the Lord is upon the waters: the God of glory thundereth..." (Psalm 29:3). Furfur, however, grants the magician the power to command such forces, symbolically inverting the divine prerogative. He is a figure of contained chaos, who when mastered, gives voice to the heavens and clarity to the human heart.

35. Marchosias, the thirty-fifth spirit, is a mighty marquis who appears as a wolf with griffon wings,

serpent's tail, and a mouth that issues flame. When compelled, he takes the form of a strong man. He is said to be loyal to the magician, truthful, and once belonged to the angelic order of Dominions before his fall. Marchosias commands legions and is a warrior spirit, often invoked in matters of defense, courage, or martial action. The reference to his former angelic status suggests a residual nobility or honor, even in his fallen state, and echoes the biblical theme of rebellious angels who once stood in the divine presence—"And the angels which kept not their first estate, but left their own habitation…" (Jude 1:6). His animal form blends symbols of strength, vision, and aggression; the flaming mouth recalls dragon imagery and perhaps the seraphim, who are literally "burning ones." Marchosias is distinguished from other infernal beings by his reputed integrity, a quality rare in the grimoires, where deception is often assumed. In this regard, he may be seen as a daemon of disciplined wrath, a guardian who fights not for dominion, but for duty. Though fallen, he is not corrupt; his allegiance, once earned, is said to be unwavering.

36. Stolas, the thirty-sixth spirit, is a powerful prince who appears in the form of a great owl before taking human shape. He is known for his command over astronomy and the teaching of celestial virtues, as well as knowledge of herbs, plants, and precious stones. Though he is not named in scripture, the owl has long stood as a symbol of hidden wisdom and nocturnal insight, as seen in classical associations with Athena and Minerva. In the Bible, owls are unclean animals, often tied to desolation

and judgment, as in *Isaiah 34:11*: "But the cormorant and the bittern shall possess it; the owl also and the raven shall dwell in it." Yet in the esoteric tradition, this very symbolism transforms the owl into a creature of the veil—one who sees in darkness and deciphers what others cannot. Stolas's teachings concern the deeper harmonies of the cosmos, offering insight into the stellar configurations that govern both macrocosmic order and microcosmic influence. His dominion over herbs and stones places him among spirits of natural magic, and his dual form suggests that wisdom must first be discerned in mystery before it is made intelligible. In ceremonial contexts, Stolas would be invoked not for base power but for gnosis—for access to the rhythm and reason embedded in the created order.

37. Phenex, the thirty-seventh spirit, is a poet among daemons. He appears in the form of a phoenix bird, singing sweetly before assuming human form at the magician's command. He is described as a hopeful spirit who was once of the angelic order and who desires to return to his rightful place in heaven after twelve centuries. His specialties include the knowledge of sciences and poetry, and he brings obedient legions. The phoenix, of course, is a mythical bird associated with resurrection, immortality, and cyclical renewal, and while not explicitly mentioned in the King James Bible, its symbolic resonance is echoed in verses such as *Job 29:18*, where the Vulgate translates, "I shall multiply my days as the phoenix." Phenex's desire to return to heaven evokes themes of repentance and restoration—common in apocryphal and mystical

texts describing the fall and potential redemption of angels. His song, like that of Orpheus, is said to be so beautiful that even infernal realms are stirred. Unlike other spirits who deceive or obscure, Phenex is a figure of clarity and artistic longing, whose presence in a magical rite may inspire eloquence, creativity, or visionary experience. He is a daemon of sacred aspiration, torn between divine memory and infernal office, singing not only to be heard but to be forgiven.

38. Halphas, the thirty-eighth spirit, is a count who manifests in the form of a stork and speaks in a hoarse voice. His role is one of war and fortification: he builds towers, fills them with weaponry, and sends men to war. Though absent from the biblical canon, the stork is a bird associated in scripture with natural instinct and migration—"Yea, the stork in the heaven knoweth her appointed times" (Jeremiah 8:7)—yet Halphas's corruption of this image casts him as a builder of strongholds not for refuge, but for conquest. His architectural role parallels biblical and ancient practices of tower-building as both defense and demonstration of human pride—recalling, in spirit if not in name, the tower of Babel. Halphas's voice, rough and unmelodious, marks a contrast to spirits like Phenex and Stolas, emphasizing function over beauty. His martial role aligns him with other spirits of conflict such as Andras and Ares, but with a focus on logistics, engineering, and preparation rather than direct violence. In magical operation, Halphas is invoked not for spontaneous chaos but for calculated campaign—he is a daemon of

infrastructure, the silent hand behind armies and armaments, whose presence signifies the imminence of force structured and sustained.

39. Malphas, the thirty-ninth spirit, is a president who appears as a crow before assuming human form. He builds houses and towers, brings knowledge of the enemy's plans, and can destroy the desires or intentions of opponents. He is also said to grant good familiars and to deceive those who offer him sacrifices unless he is constrained in a triangle. The crow form ties him to themes of omen, intelligence, and subversion; crows in folklore are messengers of death or hidden knowledge, and in scripture they appear subtly, as in *Genesis 8:7*, where Noah sends forth a raven (a corvid) as the first scout after the flood. Malphas's architectural role overlaps with Halphas, yet while the latter is a builder of war towers, Malphas is more ambiguous—constructing both edifices and deceptions. His capacity to give insight into enemies' strategies makes him akin to spirits of espionage, while his ability to sabotage hostile desires aligns him with daemons of reversal and disruption. The warning that he lies unless properly contained underscores the need for ritual precision and reinforces his trickster nature. Malphas is not merely a spirit of war or knowledge but of controlled misdirection—useful to the wise, ruinous to the incautious.

40. Raum, the fortieth spirit, is a count who manifests as a crow and then takes on human form. He is said to steal treasures from kings' houses and carry them wherever commanded, to destroy cities and dignities, to reconcile foes, and to uncover hidden

truths. Raum is unique in combining destructive power with the capacity for healing and reconciliation. His thieving nature evokes Hermes in his youthful, trickster guise, while his ability to humble rulers recalls prophetic themes of divine justice, as in *Daniel 2:21*: "He removeth kings, and setteth up kings." Though not a biblical figure, Raum channels this archetype of rebalancing power and redistributing wealth, particularly in response to injustice or hubris. His role in reconciliation is curious, given his other traits, suggesting that his chaos may be redemptive—he disrupts not for spite but to prepare the ground for something better. In magical practice, Raum serves as a spirit of subversion and strategy, one who removes obstacles by undermining the structures of power, but who can also heal the fractures that remain. He is a daemon of demolition and diplomacy, acting swiftly to tear down or repair, depending on the magician's need.

41. Focalor, the forty-first spirit, is a mighty duke who manifests in the form of a man with griffin wings. His dominion lies over winds and seas, with power to cause shipwrecks, drown men, and overthrow warships. Yet, paradoxically, he is also reputed to harm none unless commanded and is said to hope for a return to the seventh throne—an allusion likely referencing the order of Thrones among the nine angelic choirs, as understood in Christian angelology. Though he does not appear by name in the Bible, his characteristics align with divine powers over nature ascribed to God: "The sea is his, and he made it: and his hands formed the dry land"

(Psalm 95:5). Focalor's dual identity—as destroyer and penitent—renders him one of the more morally ambivalent figures in the Goetia. His control over natural forces evokes Leviathan, the primordial sea creature described in *Job 41*, and his destructive capacity mirrors the plagues and tempests sent by God as judgments throughout the Old Testament. The motif of a fallen angel who seeks restoration adds a tragic dimension to Focalor's character, casting him as more than a mere daemon of death—he is a creature of vast elemental force, caught between wrath and remembrance, destruction and deliverance.

42. Vepar, the forty-second spirit, is described as a duchess—though in many grimoires referred to with masculine pronouns—who appears as a mermaid and governs waters, guiding ships and bringing storms, decay, and disease, particularly in wounds. Vepar is not named in the scriptures but inherits much of her symbolic power from marine mythology and biblical depictions of the sea as a realm of danger and judgment. Her ability to control storms and afflict the wounded aligns with themes in *Psalm 107:25-26*: "For he commandeth, and raiseth the stormy wind... They mount up to the heaven, they go down again to the depths." The image of a mermaid further associates Vepar with seduction and mortality—a dual nature of beauty and death often assigned to sirens and sea spirits in Greco-Roman lore. Her power to manipulate the tides of battle by infecting wounds or altering maritime outcomes renders her an embodiment of the silent but pervasive forces that tip the balance of fate.

Vepar serves not as an instigator of chaos, but as a daemon of inevitability: the slow rot, the rising wave, the unexpected shift in the current that undoes even the most prepared.

43. Sabnock, the forty-third spirit, is a marquis who appears in the form of an armed soldier with a lion's head, riding a pale horse. His functions include building high towers and castles, defending them with spiritual armor, and afflicting men with festering wounds and rotting flesh. The dual nature of his craft—constructive fortification and bodily decay—places Sabnock in the realm of the guardian and the punisher. Though he is not named in the biblical canon, his characteristics echo both divine protectors and avenging agents like the angel of death in *2 Samuel 24:15-16*, where pestilence is sent upon Israel: "So the Lord sent a pestilence upon Israel... and there died of the people seventy thousand men." The lion-headed aspect connotes authority, royalty, and divine ferocity, reminiscent of the cherubim described in *Ezekiel 1*, each possessing hybrid, composite forms. The pale horse is a chilling echo of *Revelation 6:8*: "And I looked, and behold a pale horse: and his name that sat on him was Death..." Sabnock's role in spiritual warfare is thus comprehensive—he builds defenses but also afflicts enemies, tests the integrity of flesh, and marks the corruptible nature of all fortifications. In magical rites, he is invoked for protection, strength, and ruinous judgment, depending on the will of the operator.

44. Shan, often rendered as Shax, is the forty-fourth spirit and a great marquis who takes the form of a

stork with a raucous voice. He is said to rob kings of their senses, steal money out of houses, and deliver horses to the magician. Most notably, he may deceive unless confined in a triangle, and even then may speak truth only intermittently. Shax also has the power to take away sight, hearing, and understanding, making him a spirit of illusion, theft, and disruption. He may be compared to the adversarial forces described in *2 Thessalonians 2:11*: "And for this cause God shall send them strong delusion, that they should believe a lie." His bird form, combined with vocal disharmony, suggests an inversion of divine messengers—where angels announce peace and clarity, Shax distorts perception and misleads judgment. He operates in the gray realm between revelation and deception, a daemon whose gifts are conditional and potentially treacherous. His ability to bestow horses—symbols of speed and war—parallels the provision of tools that may be misused or turn against the wielder. Shax represents the necessity of ritual precision and ethical constraint, for without mastery, his tricks can destroy both magician and intended target alike.

45. Viné, the forty-fifth spirit, is a king and earl who appears in the form of a lion riding a black horse and bearing a viper in his hand. He is said to reveal secrets of the past, present, and future, and to uncover hidden things. He also builds towers, destroys walls, and causes storms. Although his name has no clear biblical equivalent, his function resonates with the divine attribute of revealing hidden things, as seen in *Daniel 2:22*: "He revealeth the deep and secret things: he knoweth what is in

the darkness." The lion symbolism recalls both nobility and divine wrath; the black horse may evoke the horse of famine in *Revelation 6:5-6*, and the viper conjures themes of cunning, poison, and revelation with risk. Viné's power to destroy walls and call down storms suggests an apocalyptic character—an undoer of strongholds, not merely physical but symbolic. He is a kingly force of clarity wrapped in terror, whose wisdom is inseparable from upheaval. Viné's insights are not granted passively but through confrontation with forces that shake, break, and expose. He may be invoked for profound revelation, but what is uncovered may also bring ruin or irreversible change.

46. Bifrons, the forty-sixth spirit, is an earl who appears first as a monstrous entity before assuming human form. He is described as possessing the power to move corpses from their graves, illuminate the sciences and arts, and reveal the properties of herbs, stones, and planetary influences. His necromantic role places him in proximity to the more chthonic daemons of the Goetia, whose power lies in the liminal space between the living and the dead. Although not named in the Bible, Bifrons embodies themes explicitly condemned in scripture, particularly in *Deuteronomy 18:10-11*: "There shall not be found among you... a consulter with familiar spirits, or a wizard, or a necromancer." Yet in magical contexts, Bifrons is a bearer of ancient knowledge—of graves, stars, and secret traditions—offering insights buried not only in tombs but in the hidden strata of time and memory. His name may derive from Janus Bifrons, the two-faced Roman

god who looked both to the past and future, which aligns with Bifrons's ability to interpret planetary alignments and ancient secrets. In ceremonial practice, he would be summoned not merely for the unsettling power to shift the dead, but for the philosophical and astrological understanding that transcends death and links human intellect to the broader cosmos.

47. Vual, also spelled Voval, is the forty-seventh spirit and is ranked as a duke. He is said to appear as a large camel before taking on human form and speaks in an obscure Egyptian tongue. His powers include procuring the love of women, especially widows, and facilitating romantic alliances between friends and foes. He is also said to give true answers concerning the past, present, and future. Though not cited in the Bible, the camel is frequently used in scripture to represent wealth and endurance, as in *Genesis 24*, where camels are central to the story of Isaac and Rebekah's betrothal. However, in Vual's case, the camel form is an initial concealment—a symbol of long journeys, burdens, or even the mysteries of the desert, suggesting a daemonic presence associated with hidden knowledge and emotional manipulation. His speech in an "Egyptian tongue" points to arcane wisdom or forgotten languages, imbuing him with an exotic mystique often associated with Egyptian theology and love spells. Vual's romantic influence, especially over women grieving or alone, suggests a spirit who exploits vulnerability but also facilitates emotional connections—complex, morally ambivalent functions that make him as useful as he is potentially

deceptive. He is a daemon of persuasion and temporal insight, whose workings must be discerned carefully lest desire masquerade as destiny.

48. Haagenti, the forty-eighth spirit, is a president who manifests as a mighty bull with griffin wings before transforming into a human sage. He is renowned for his power to transmute metals into gold and water into wine—clear allusions to the alchemical and Eucharistic transformations that sit at the heart of both esoteric philosophy and Christian mystery. Although Haagenti does not appear in the Bible by name, his miraculous capabilities strongly echo Christ's first miracle at Cana: "Jesus saith unto them, Fill the waterpots with water… and they bare it. When the ruler of the feast had tasted the water that was made wine…" (John 2:7-9). Haagenti's acts of transformation align him with the archetype of the philosopher's stone—transmutation not merely of base metals, but of the soul. His dual form—as bull and as winged creature—combines the raw strength of earth with the airy nobility of divine insight. In magical operations, Haagenti is not invoked for spectacle but for elevation: the raising of consciousness through the mastery of change. He may offer material gain, but his deeper gift is the internalization of transformation itself. He is a daemon of wisdom cloaked in mystery, embodying the synthesis of strength and subtlety.

49. Crocell, the forty-ninth spirit, is a duke who appears in the form of an angel speaking mystic truths. He is said to teach the liberal sciences, produce great noises akin to rushing waters, and reveal the

locations of natural springs and hidden waters. Though not found in canonical scripture, Crocell's attributes recall the biblical association of divine voice and water, particularly in *Ezekiel 43:2*: "His voice was like a noise of many waters." As a teacher of hidden springs, Crocell may be understood as a psychopompic figure who reveals both physical and spiritual sources of renewal. His connection to the element of water also associates him with emotion, intuition, and purification, central concepts in mystical theologies and mystery schools. The idea of hidden springs often symbolizes access to concealed wisdom or spiritual vitality, and Crocell's role in their revelation marks him as a spirit of illumination. His angelic appearance underscores this, as does his gift for teaching the classical disciplines, positioning him among the daemons of enlightenment and sound. Though not necessarily malevolent, Crocell is a liminal figure—his great noise may awaken, inspire, or overwhelm—and he must be approached with respect for the waters he stirs.

50. Furcas, the fiftieth spirit, is a knight who rides a pale horse and bears a sharp weapon. He is said to teach philosophy, astronomy, astrology, logic, chiromancy, and pyromancy—encompassing a broad array of occult and classical disciplines. While his name is not scriptural, the pale horse is a potent biblical image: "And I looked, and behold a pale horse: and his name that sat on him was Death..." (Revelation 6:8). However, Furcas's function is not death, but instruction—especially in disciplines that interpret both the stars and the self. He is a daemon of wisdom rather than judgment, whose weapon is

clarity of mind rather than destruction. His dominion over chiromancy and pyromancy links him to the elemental arts, and his authority in logic and philosophy suggests a deeply structured intelligence. Furcas is not a deceiver but a systematizer—one who imposes order upon mystery through study. His role in magical operation is that of the professor or elder sage, a knight of the intellect who defends through precision and understanding. Whether one seeks insight into destiny or illumination of the heavens, Furcas is a guide across the terrain of reason and revelation alike.

51. Balam, the fifty-first spirit, is a mighty and terrible king who appears with three heads: that of a bull, a man, and a ram. He speaks with a deep, commanding voice and rides a fierce bear, carrying a hawk upon his fist. He is said to grant perfect answers concerning the past, present, and future, as well as providing the power of invisibility and wit. Though not identical in spelling, Balam is often associated with Balaam, the prophet of *Numbers 22-24*, who is hired to curse Israel but instead blesses them under divine compulsion. The King James Version recalls: "And God said unto Balaam, Thou shalt not go with them; thou shalt not curse the people: for they are blessed" (Numbers 22:12). While Balaam was a complex figure—both diviner and false prophet—Balam in the Goetia has shed any pious veneer and become a composite figure of judgment and preternatural knowledge. His triune head suggests command over multiple aspects of nature or reality, blending fertility (ram), strength

(bull), and reason (man). The hawk and bear imagery enhance this symbolic constellation—visionary precision and brute force. Balam is a lord of temporal insight, one whose truths are fearsome not because they deceive, but because they reveal with unrelenting certainty.

52. Alloces, the fifty-second spirit, is a duke who appears as a soldier riding a great horse, with the face of a lion, flaming eyes, and a thunderous voice. He teaches astronomy and the liberal sciences and commands a considerable host. Though not present in canonical scripture, his leonine aspect and fiery nature recall angelic descriptions in apocalyptic texts, particularly the cherubic visions of *Ezekiel 1*, where "every one had four faces... and they had the hands of a man under their wings... and their appearance was like burning coals of fire." Alloces's authority in astronomy positions him among the intelligences of the celestial spheres, akin to the Archangel Raziel or Hermes Trismegistus in other traditions. His thunderous voice signals the delivery of unmediated truth—divine or infernal—and his martial form emphasizes the active enforcement of intellectual dominion. He is a daemon not merely of knowledge, but of its discipline and enforcement. When summoned in ceremonial practice, Alloces may serve as a master of order in the realm of intellectual pursuit, structuring the chaos of thought through the lens of celestial law. Though fierce in aspect, his loyalty to the sciences affirms that even in fire and fury, there may dwell clarity.

53. Camio, also rendered Caim, is the fifty-third spirit, a president who initially appears as a blackbird or

thrush before taking on human form bearing a sharp sword. He is renowned for his ability to communicate perfectly in all languages, understand the voices of birds, dogs, and oxen, and to answer truly concerning things to come. The image of the blackbird recalls the prophetic nature of omens, as birds are often used as signs in both classical and biblical literature. His linguistic powers mirror the reversal of Babel, where language once divided mankind—"Therefore is the name of it called Babel... the Lord did there confound the language of all the earth" (Genesis 11:9). Camio, by contrast, restores unity through communication, making him a daemon of divination, eloquence, and interspecies understanding. The sharp sword he bears may symbolize the incisive nature of his truth—piercing and precise. His faculty to interpret animal voices positions him uniquely among the Goetic spirits as a master of hidden speech and natural signs. In practice, he is invoked not only for divinatory insight but for translation between realms—between man and beast, symbol and language, present and future. He is a spirit of decipherment, where truth lies waiting to be heard from all corners of creation.

54. Murmur, the fifty-fourth spirit, is both a duke and earl, appearing as a soldier riding a vulture, crowned with a ducal coronet, and preceded by a retinue of trumpets. He speaks with a grave and authoritative tone and is said to teach philosophy and summon the souls of the dead to answer questions. His name, echoing the sound of low utterance or ritual chant, suggests both invocation and resonance. While not found in scripture by

name, his necromantic role places him near those figures condemned in *Deuteronomy 18:11* and *Isaiah 8:19*: "Should not a people seek unto their God? for the living to the dead?" Murmur's grandeur, however, sets him apart from mere conjurer spirits; he embodies a funerary dignity, a spirit of rites and ancestral knowledge rather than chaos. The vulture, often symbolic of death and purification, and the trumpet procession—which conjures *1 Thessalonians 4:16*: "For the Lord himself shall descend from heaven with a shout, with the voice of the archangel, and with the trump of God…"—suggest his operations exist at the boundary between death and revelation. Murmur governs not merely the act of summoning, but the ceremonial gravity that makes the dead speak with purpose.

55. Orobas, the fifty-fifth spirit, is a powerful prince who appears first as a horse before taking human form. He is deeply revered for his honesty and faithfulness, providing truthful answers about the past, present, and future, and granting favor with friends and foes alike. He also protects against temptation from other spirits and ensures that the magician is not deceived. Unlike many Goetic entities who demand strict constraint to avoid deceit, Orobas is said to be inherently trustworthy—a remarkable exception. Though he bears no biblical name, his virtue aligns him more with the guardian angelic type than with infernal deceivers. His equine form connotes nobility, speed, and loyalty, much like the white horse of Revelation: "And I saw heaven opened, and behold a white horse; and he that sat upon him was called Faithful

and True..." (Revelation 19:11). In this symbolic mirror, Orobas may be understood as a reflection of divine intelligences who remained uncorrupted. As a spirit who bestows favor and truth without duplicity, Orobas is among the most favored daemons in magical tradition—sought not for domination, but for counsel. He stands as a spirit of integrity in a system full of manipulation, a bearer of divine echo rather than infernal fraud.

56. Gremory, the fifty-sixth spirit, is a strong duke who appears in the form of a beautiful woman riding a great camel and wearing a duchess's crown. He is said to discover hidden treasures, answer truthfully about the past, present, and future, and procure the love of women. While bearing a feminine form, Gremory is considered masculine in rank and energy within the Goetic hierarchy. His presence evokes themes of androgyny and liminality, particularly relevant in esoteric traditions where divine and daemonic figures often blend gendered traits to signify power beyond material duality. The camel upon which he rides is an ancient symbol of endurance and wealth, a creature of the desert whose ability to traverse barren places speaks to Gremory's skill in uncovering what is concealed or forgotten. Though he is not referenced directly in the Bible, his capacity to reveal hidden treasures recalls verses like *Isaiah 45:3*: "And I will give thee the treasures of darkness, and hidden riches of secret places." Gremory's love-inducing powers, especially upon women, suggest mastery over Venusian and lunar forces, making him particularly potent in workings involving romantic influence,

attraction, and emotional revelation. Yet his crown and high status also affirm his sovereignty over secrets—those of love, wealth, and prophecy alike.

57. Ose, the fifty-seventh spirit, is a president who appears as a leopard before transforming into a man. He is said to give true answers regarding divine and secret matters, to confer wisdom in all liberal sciences, and—most notably—to induce delusion, causing individuals to believe themselves to be kings or popes or to suffer identity confusion for extended periods. Though not found in scripture, Ose's talents resonate with the biblical theme of God blinding or confounding the proud, as seen in *Romans 1:22*: "Professing themselves to be wise, they became fools." His leopard form suggests speed, stealth, and predatory intelligence—qualities that align with his function as both enlightener and deceiver. Ose's manipulation of perception is a sobering reminder of the thin veil between insight and madness. His gifts, when sought ethically, can confer profound philosophical knowledge; but when misapplied or approached without clarity of purpose, his delusions can lead to ruin. He is a spirit of paradox: both a teacher of truth and an agent of misbelief. In ceremonial invocation, one must approach him with disciplined intent, lest his power to reshape reality turn inward and fragment the seeker's own mind.

58. Amy, the fifty-eighth spirit, is a president who initially appears as a blazing flame before taking human shape. He is said to teach astronomy and the liberal sciences, grant familiar spirits, and reveal treasures guarded by spirits. Additionally, Amy was

once part of the angelic order of powers, and he retains a desire to return to the Seventh Heaven. Though his name is not found in the Bible, the image of a fiery, fallen being seeking restoration echoes the broader Christian mythos of the rebel angels and particularly the fall of Lucifer, whose brilliance is described in *Isaiah 14:12*: "How art thou fallen from heaven, O Lucifer, son of the morning!" Amy's flame-form recalls the fiery presence of divine messengers, such as those seen in the burning bush of *Exodus 3*, and his teaching role links him to the angelic archetype of the Watchers, some of whom taught humanity hidden knowledge in the Book of Enoch. His grant of familiar spirits suggests power over intermediary beings or astral intelligences, a potent aid to the magician but also a significant responsibility. Amy represents both lost glory and enduring brilliance—his fire is not entirely quenched, and when summoned properly, he may illuminate paths both ancient and hidden.

59. Orias, the fifty-ninth spirit, is a marquis who appears as a lion riding a strong horse with a serpent's tail and bearing two hissing serpents in his hands. He is said to teach the virtues of the stars, the mansions of the planets, and the mechanics of planetary motion. He grants dignity, favor, and the goodwill of friends and foes, and he confers titles of honor. Though not named in the canonical Bible, his lion-like form and astrological mastery align him with celestial kingship and solar influence. The lion, as seen in *Proverbs 28:1*, symbolizes strength and boldness: "The wicked flee when no man pursueth: but the righteous are bold as a lion." Orias's serpents

represent dual wisdom and danger—linked to both the Edenic tempter and to symbols of healing, as in the brazen serpent of *Numbers 21:9*. As a master of astrological knowledge, Orias reveals the inner workings of fate and influence, equipping the magician with understanding of planetary timing, ritual power, and ceremonial timing. His ability to bestow high rank and reconcile adversaries speaks to his function as an occult diplomat and cosmological interpreter. He is a spirit of noble bearing and celestial negotiation, one whose power is not brute but harmonized with the movement of the heavens.

60. Vapula, the sixtieth spirit, is a duke who appears in the form of a lion with griffin wings. He is said to teach philosophy, mechanical arts, and sciences, including handicrafts and trades. Vapula's focus on practical knowledge and skill distinguishes him among the Goetia as a patron of artisans, builders, and thinkers. Though he does not appear in the Bible, his role recalls the wisdom endowed to Bezalel, the craftsman of the Tabernacle: "And I have filled him with the spirit of God, in wisdom, and in understanding, and in knowledge, and in all manner of workmanship" (Exodus 31:3). Vapula's leonine and griffinic form suggests both physical and intellectual dominion—courage merged with far-reaching vision. His influence is not abstract but applied, reinforcing the esoteric truth that mastery of the material world is itself a spiritual achievement. As such, he is invoked by those seeking to refine their technical skills, build enduring structures, or complete great works.

Vapula's knowledge uplifts the tradesman and dignifies the craftsman, embodying the principle that work is sacred when aligned with divine order and executed with excellence.

61. Zagan, the sixty-first spirit, is a great king and president who appears first as a bull with griffin wings, later taking on human form. He is said to make men witty, turn wine into water and blood into wine, and transform any metal into coinage. In his dual aspects of transformation and wit, Zagan bears marks of both the trickster and the philosopher-king. Although his name is not found in biblical texts, his powers recall Christ's first miracle at Cana—transforming water into wine (John 2:9)—and the various references throughout scripture where divine agency manipulates the natural elements. More subtly, Zagan's transmutational skills evoke the alchemical ideal of *solve et coagula*: to break down and reform. His ability to bestow wit and sharp intelligence marks him as a daemon of both cunning and clarity, making him useful in endeavors requiring rhetorical or intellectual finesse. At the same time, his power over matter implies a deep understanding of the mutable nature of the physical world, placing him in proximity to the divine artisans of the Old Testament—those who wrought gold, silver, and precious vessels for sacred purposes. Zagan's knowledge straddles the metaphysical and practical, alchemical and comedic, rendering him both a sage and a subverter.

62. Valac, the sixty-second spirit, is a president who appears as a small boy with angel's wings, riding a two-headed dragon. He is known to deliver true

answers about hidden treasures and to reveal the location of serpents. The contrast between his childlike appearance and his formidable dragon mount introduces a duality of innocence and danger—an image common to esoteric and apocalyptic literature. Though Valac does not appear by name in scripture, his imagery draws upon deeply biblical motifs: serpents, dragons, and hidden wisdom. The two-headed dragon echoes *Revelation 12*, where a great red dragon threatens the woman clothed with the sun. Meanwhile, the child figure mounted upon it suggests mastery over primal forces rather than submission to them. Valac's association with serpents may also link him to Moses's brazen serpent in *Numbers 21:9*, an object of healing when seen by faith. As a revealer of hidden things, especially underground or guarded by reptiles, Valac occupies the role of psychopomp or guide into the underworld—one who uncovers what is buried, protected, or cursed. He embodies the paradox of purity guiding power, a small figure astride the monstrous, whose knowledge is subtle and serpentine.

63. Andras, the sixty-third spirit, is a mighty marquis who manifests in the form of an angel with the head of an owl, riding a black wolf and wielding a sharp sword. He is described as a dangerous spirit who sows discord among people and kills those in positions of authority if the magician is not careful. Although unnamed in the biblical canon, Andras's function parallels the "spirit of division" described in *Luke 12:51*: "Suppose ye that I am come to give

peace on earth? I tell you, Nay; but rather division." His owl head signals nocturnal wisdom or hidden sight, but also serves as a traditional symbol of ill omen, while the black wolf evokes untamed aggression and wilderness. In total, Andras is a daemon of destructive cunning, a force that tears apart alliances and undermines structure, particularly when provoked or mishandled. His sword and wolf mount denote martial authority and death, emphasizing the need for strict control when dealing with him. He is not a spirit of transformation or enlightenment, but of entropy, ruin, and political disarray. For those seeking to disrupt unjust power structures or sever dangerous ties, Andras may be potent, but his path is one strewn with wreckage.

64. Haures, also called Flauros, is the sixty-fourth spirit, a mighty duke who first appears as a terrifying leopard, engulfed in flames, before taking human form. He speaks truthfully of past, present, and future, but only when bound within a magical triangle. He is also said to burn and destroy the magician's enemies and has power to protect against other spirits. Haures is a fiery avenger, not merely a diviner. His leopard form suggests speed, elegance, and lethality, and his fiery appearance recalls the burning ones of *Isaiah 6:2-6*, the seraphim, whose flames signify divine presence and judgment. His refusal to speak truth unless properly constrained reinforces the ceremonial necessity of magical boundaries—especially the triangle, which in Western esotericism represents containment of infernal forces and elevation of divine will. Like

Elijah calling down fire upon the altar, Haures is invoked in contexts of righteous vengeance and purification by flame. His dual role—both oracular and annihilating—renders him a force of revelatory destruction. Though dangerous, he is not without honor; he does not deceive when properly constrained and acts with integrity under direction. Haures is a daemon of controlled fire, a bearer of burning truth and targeted wrath.

65. Andrealphus, the sixty-fifth spirit, is a mighty marquis who appears first as a peacock before assuming human shape. He is said to teach astronomy and geometry and to transform men into birds. The peacock is a traditional symbol of vanity, immortality, and divine vision—its tail a mimic of the stars. In this form, Andrealphus connects celestial understanding with aesthetic grandeur. While his name does not appear in the biblical canon, the peacock's symbolic legacy stretches from the Persian Simurgh to the Christian adaptation as a symbol of resurrection. His transformative powers—changing men into birds—invoke shamanic traditions of flight, spiritual ascent, and escape from the confines of flesh. He is a daemonic teacher of the heavens, of measurement and proportion, and of the beauty within cosmic order. His alignment with astronomy and geometry aligns him with the Platonic view of the universe as structured by divine ratios, echoing the sentiment of *Wisdom of Solomon 11:20* (Deuterocanon): "Thou hast ordered all things in measure and number and weight." Andrealphus offers intellectual elevation, but his peacock form cautions the

magician against pride. He invites the soul to rise, but also tempts it to admire its own wings too long in the mirror of knowledge.

66. Cimejes, also spelled Cimeies or Kimaris, is the sixty-sixth spirit, a marquis who appears as a valiant warrior riding a black horse. He is said to teach grammar, logic, and rhetoric, to discover hidden treasures, and to command spirits in Africa. Though his name does not appear in the canonical Bible, his association with language and learning aligns him with the angelic teachers of early biblical and apocryphal literature, such as those in the *Book of Enoch* who taught humanity various arts and sciences. His equestrian image suggests martial nobility and command, while the black horse echoes the apocalyptic symbol of famine or control from *Revelation 6:5*: "And I beheld, and lo a black horse; and he that sat on him had a pair of balances in his hand." However, in Cimejes, this symbol transforms from judgment to mastery, especially over language and knowledge. His role in teaching the trivium—grammar, logic, and rhetoric—positions him as a daemon of classical learning and intellectual elegance. Additionally, his dominion over spirits in Africa implies a historical intersection with regional spiritual systems, perhaps referencing the diffusion of magical knowledge across continents. Cimejes is a teacher, rider, and commander—a spirit who harnesses intellect and speech as both weapon and gift.

67. Amdusias, the sixty-seventh spirit, is a duke who appears initially as a unicorn before taking human form. He is most famously associated with causing

musical instruments to sound without human hands and is said to command a noisy and infernal orchestra. He can also cause trees to bend and incline at will. Though not named in scripture, his presence conjures a hybrid of biblical symbolism and Dionysian spectacle. The unicorn, while often mythologized, is referenced in the King James Bible as a symbol of wild strength: "God brought them out of Egypt; he hath as it were the strength of an unicorn" (Numbers 23:22). Amdusias's command of music without physical contact suggests invisible harmonies, a daemon of resonance and vibration whose influence reaches into the auditory dimensions of magic. His capacity to move trees may symbolize an influence over nature itself, echoing psalms where "the trees of the field shall clap their hands" (Isaiah 55:12). In ceremonial practice, Amdusias is invoked for musical inspiration, unseen forces, and psychic movement—his songs are not of comfort, but of awe. He is a spirit of sound as power, of music as command, and of beauty that bends the world to its cadence.

68. Belial, the sixty-eighth spirit, is one of the most powerful and infamous names in demonological literature. He appears as two beautiful angels seated in a chariot of fire and speaks with a seductive eloquence. Created next after Lucifer, Belial is said to have fallen along with him and to be the embodiment of lawlessness, seduction, and corruption. He bestows high titles and grants the favor of friends and enemies alike, but only when sacrifices or offerings are made. Belial is one of the few spirits named explicitly in the Bible: "What

concord hath Christ with Belial?" (2 Corinthians 6:15), and earlier in *Deuteronomy 13:13*, where "children of Belial" are rebellious men who lead others to idolatry. His name itself may be translated as "worthless" or "lawless." In the Goetia, however, Belial is presented not as a mere tempter, but as a king of power, status, and influence, whose gifts are real but whose allegiance is dangerous. His dual angelic form suggests a counterfeit beauty, echoing Paul's warning that "Satan himself is transformed into an angel of light" (2 Corinthians 11:14). Belial is thus not only a spirit of ascent, but of compromise—a being who offers thrones built on corrupted altars.

69. Decarabia, the sixty-ninth spirit, is a marquis who appears as a pentacle-shaped star before taking human form. He is said to reveal the virtues of herbs and precious stones, control birds and other animals, and transform reality through natural correspondences. Though not found in scripture, Decarabia's powers draw heavily from natural magic, in which plants, minerals, and animals hold spiritual or medicinal significance. His pentacle form is particularly notable, symbolizing the microcosm of man, the harmony of the elements, and the fivefold symmetry of nature itself. In Hermetic and Pythagorean traditions, the pentagram is a symbol of divine proportion and cosmic alignment—suggesting that Decarabia appears not just as a shape, but as a living glyph of universal balance. His dominion over birds recalls the biblical image of creation's stewardship and may reflect an animistic sensitivity to divine order within the living world. Decarabia is thus a spirit of

nature's secret virtues—not for destruction or illusion, but for the harmonization of man with the natural and astral worlds. His knowledge lies in the alignment of elements, the enchantment of stone and leaf, and the subtle science of resonance and flight.

70. Seere, the seventieth spirit, is a mighty prince who appears as a beautiful man riding a winged horse, reminiscent of the mythical Pegasus. He is said to move swiftly from place to place, bringing things to pass in an instant and delivering answers concerning treasure, theft, or hidden knowledge. Though not named in the Bible, Seere's rapidity and winged steed connect him to divine messengers such as the cherubim or the horsemen of *Zechariah 6*, who patrol the earth at God's command. In magical literature, his neutral alignment and benevolent character set him apart: Seere neither deceives nor compels. He performs his tasks faithfully and without requiring payment or offering harm. This makes him one of the few Goetic spirits regarded as wholly trustworthy—a rare trait in the infernal catalogue. His role is often practical: recovering lost items, discovering truth, and facilitating movement, both physical and metaphysical. As a daemon of speed, vision, and reliability, Seere is invoked not to dominate but to assist. His presence in ritual is like a sudden wind—gentle or strong, but always purposeful—carrying with it the certainty that what is sought shall swiftly come to pass.

71. Dantalion, the seventy-first spirit, is a powerful duke who appears as a man with many faces—of both

men and women—each of which speaks in a different tongue. He holds in his hand a book, the source of his knowledge, and is said to know all human thoughts, grant wisdom in all arts and sciences, and sway the minds and affections of others at will. His polyfacial form suggests mastery over language, culture, and psychology—an embodiment of diversity and internal multiplicity. While not named in the biblical canon, Dantalion's attributes echo the spiritual insight of Solomon, whose heart "was as the sand that is on the sea shore" (1 Kings 4:29), encompassing manifold understanding. The image of the many-faced figure recalls mystical depictions of divine omniscience, while his open book connects him with the archetype of the sage or scribe—one who not only knows, but can teach. His dominion over emotion and thought renders him a spirit of persuasion, ideal for workings of influence, negotiation, and reconciliation. Yet his faculty is not solely manipulative; he may also be invoked to aid in introspection, as he sees clearly into the hidden recesses of the heart. Dantalion is a daemon of complex unity—his faces are legion, but his purpose is singular: to comprehend and communicate what lies within.

72. Andromalius, the seventy-second and final spirit, is an earl who appears as a man holding a large serpent. He is chiefly tasked with uncovering theft, recovering stolen goods, revealing hidden wickedness, and punishing thieves and deceivers. Unlike many other spirits in the Goetia, Andromalius is judicial in character—a daemon of

righteous retribution and concealed justice. While his name is absent from scripture, his attributes recall the moral vengeance of the Old Testament prophets and the eschatological judgments of Revelation. The serpent he bears suggests both the cunning of the deceiver and the vigilance of one who sees what others cannot. Andromalius exposes hypocrisy and punishes treachery, acting almost as an infernal agent of divine justice. In this, he parallels figures like the angel in *Zechariah 5:3*, who enforces the curse that "shall enter into the house of the thief." Andromalius is invoked not to manipulate, but to correct—to reveal what has been hidden, to return what has been unlawfully taken, and to exact a moral balance in the unseen world. As the last in the hierarchy, he stands as the terminus of power, a daemon of closure and consequence. He is the reckoner, the final word, the sword that follows the whisper.